The Jeffries Duet Concertina Tutor

Gary Coover

Rollston Press

The Jeffries Duet Concertina Tutor
by Gary Coover

All rights reserved. No part of this book may be reproduced, scanned, transmitted or distributed in any printed or electronic form without the prior permission of the author except in the case of brief quotations embodied in articles or reviews.

Copyright © 2020 Gary Coover

ISBN-13: 978-1-7326121-7-4

All titles are traditional or in the public domain unless otherwise noted.
All arrangements and transcriptions by Gary Coover unless otherwise noted.

Also by Gary Coover: *Anglo Concertina in the Harmonic Style* (2013)
Christmas Concertina (2013)
Civil War Concertina (2014)
Easy Anglo 1-2-3 (2015)
75 Irish Session Tunes for Anglo Concertina (2015)
The Pocket Shantyman (2017)
Pirate Songs for Concertina (2018)
Cowboy Concertina (2018)
Sailor Songs for Concertina (2019)

Front Cover Photo by Paul Woloschuk (www.paulwoloschukphotography.uk)

ROLLSTON PRESS
1717 Ala Wai Blvd #1703
Honolulu, HI 96815
USA
info@rollstonpress.com

TABLE OF CONTENTS

PREFACE 6
INTRODUCTION 7
HISTORY 8
THE RAMPIN' CAT 9
THE INSTRUMENT 10
KEYBOARD 12
TABLATURE 17
RIGHT HAND MELODY 18
ACCOMPANIMENT TECHNIQUES 20
LEFT HAND CHORDS 22
PLAYING IN DIFFERENT KEYS 29
WHAT IF MY DUET IS IN A DIFFERENT HOME KEY? 30
ANGLO VS JEFFRIES DUET 31
WHAT OTHER JEFFRIES DUET PLAYERS SAY 32
TUNES 33
    Mary Had a Little Lamb 35
    Poor Old Horse (C) 36
    Poor Old Horse (G) 37
    Oh Susanna 38
    Twinkle Twinkle Little Star 39
    Frere Jacques 40
    Pop Goes the Weasel 41
    Variations on Shepherd's Hey 42
    Logan Water 44
    Flow Gently Sweet Afton 45
    Amazing Grace 46
    Oh Susanna (chords) 47
    Young Collins 48
    The Man in the Moon 50
    King Pharim 52
    Furusato 53
    The Whaleman's Lament 54
    The Cowman's Prayer 55
    Rose of the Redlands 56
    Auld Lang Syne 58
    The Blue-Eyed Stranger 59
    Weeping, Sad and Lonely 60
    The Star of the County Down 62

Miss Smith's Morris	64
Galopede	66
In the Bleak Midwinter	68
Loch Lomond	69
Salmontails Up the Water	70
The Quaker's Wife	72
Kate's Rambles	73
The Gurnard Waltz	74
Alfred Montmarquette's 6/8	76
Country Gardens	78
Shenandoah	79
In Dulci Jubilo	80
The Mudgee Waltz	81
Eleanor Plunkett	82
Rights of Man	83
The Queen's Delight	84
Da Slockit Light	86
American Boot Dance	88
Peter's Peerie Boat	90
Procrastination Waltz	92
Dearest Dickie	94
The Battle of the Somme	95
Old Magnolia	96
Merry Month of May	97
Red Wing	98
Gärdebylåten	100
A Mighty Fortress is Our God	102
Londonderry Air	103
Hell Ship	104
Portsmouth (Setting 1)	106
Portsmouth (Setting 2)	108
The Indian Queen	109
Auld Donald	110
Three Around Three	111
What a Friend We Have in Jesus	112
Gathering Peascods	114
The American Patrol	116
Angeline the Baker (D)	118
Angeline the Baker (C)	119
Orkney Rope Waltz	120
Minuet in G	122
How Great Thou Art	123
My Wild Irish Rose	124
When Irish Eyes Are Smiling	128
Kojo no Tsuki	132
Nottingham Castle	133
Beer That Tastes Like Beer	134

Under the Anheuser Busch 136
St. James Infirmary 140
Let Me Call You Sweetheart 142
Land of Hope & Glory 146
The Entertainer 148
Goodbye, Good Luck, God Bless You 150
When You Know You're Not Forgotten by the Girl You Can't Forget 154
Christ the Lord is Risen Today 158
Fur Elise 159
My Old Dutch 160
The Liberty Bell March 162
The Cross of Inverness 164
I Do Like to be Beside the Seaside 166
After You've Gone 170
La Partida 172
Bourrée in E minor 174
Pavane 176
They Needed a Songbird in Heaven 179
Minuet in D Minor 182

VIDEOS & RECORDINGS 184
THE AUTHOR 192
ACKNOWLEDGEMENTS & THANKS 193
ALPHABETICAL LIST OF TUNES 194

PREFACE

When I first became interested in British and Irish traditional music, and in particular the music of the concertina, it was a treat to discover the many wonderful recordings on the Free Reed record label run by concertina collector Neil Wayne.

Although I was familiar with Anglo and English concertinas, I quickly learned there were other systems like Maccann Duets and Crane Duets. But the one recording that really got my attention was *The Rampin' Cat* by Michael Hebbert, featuring something called a Jeffries Duet concertina.

What an amazing sound it had! Melody plus accompaniment plus complex chords plus bass runs, and all coming from one little concertina making an enormous sound.

Needless to say, I instantly decided I had to have a concertina that could sound like that.

A Jeffries Duet subsequently turned up for sale in England and I bought it sight unseen. Imagine my excitement at finally receiving the package covered in strange stamps and customs seals, opening it up, getting the concertina out of its beat-up leather case, picking it up, trying a button here and there, and then realizing I hadn't a clue how to play it. Absolutely nothing made sense.

So, I got a pen and paper, drew a bunch of circles, and sat down at a piano to try to figure out what button was what note. Made even more difficult since the tuning wasn't in modern pitch! Finally done, I stared at the paper for a long time and still couldn't make heads or tails of it.

And, I didn't know anybody who had a Jeffries Duet, or had even heard of one, and there were no books or teachers available anywhere.

Thus began my journey learning to play the Jeffries Duet – completely lost!

After much trial and error, a lot of perseverance, and an untold number of missteps and mistakes, patterns eventually emerged that slowly turned into recognizable tunes.

Today, after all that initial anguish, I find the Jeffries Duet is just tremendous fun to play. Octaves, harmonies, oom-pahs, fancy chords – all can be brought to bear for almost any tune, slow or fast, expressive or bombastic. There's just something about the Jeffries Duet that sets it apart from the other duets, always exciting and never boring. It's a great instrument for folk tunes, classical tunes, church hymns, old pop standards, Gilded-Age and Tin Pan Alley songs, perhaps even jazz, blues, avant-garde and experimental music.

Many of the tunes in the book include QR code links to videos so you can see and hear how the tune is played, and there are also QR code links to videos and recordings by other Jeffries Duet players. These videos, and others as they become available, can be found on the "Jeffries Duet" playlist on the Angloconc channel on YouTube.

At full steam, a Jeffries Duet with "octaves in the right and fistfuls of chords in the left" is an amazing sight to hear and behold.

I hope this book helps you get started on your way.

INTRODUCTION

The concertina is a remarkably unusual bellows-powered music-making machine full of buttons, levers, springs, pads and wind-powered vibrating metal reeds. First patented by Sir Charles Wheatstone in 1829, there are now a variety of different types of concertina that at first glance appear to look the same - they all have wooden or metal ends with 6, 8 or 12 sides, little round buttons on each end, folding leather bellows in between, and they make sounds when buttons are pressed and the two ends are either pushed or pulled by hand.

That's where the similarity ends.

If it has hand straps, two or three horizontal rows of buttons that play a different note pushing or pulling, it is called an "Anglo" concertina. This is the most common type of concertina, typically with 20 or 30 buttons, or more.

If it has little thumbstraps and pinkie rests, four vertical rows of buttons on each end, and the buttons play the same note pushing and pulling, it is an "English" concertina. Typically with 48 to 64 buttons equally divided between the two sides.

If it has hand straps and the buttons play the same note pushing and pulling, then it is most likely a type of duet concertina, so named because the two sides can be played independently of one another, often for melody on the right side and accompaniment on the left side.

Duets are fairly rare instruments, the most common having six vertical rows is called a "Maccann" Duet, and a lesser known one with five vertical rows is called a "Crane" or "Triumph" Duet. They might have as few as 35 buttons or as many as 81 buttons.

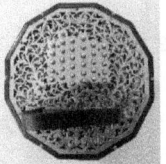

And then there's the "Jeffries" Duet.

It is an incredibly rare instrument that for all intents and purposes looks like an Anglo concertina, but it has <u>four</u> horizontal rows with each button playing the same note whether pushed or pulled.

Jeffries Duets vary in size from 27 buttons to 77 buttons and are the only duets based around a home key that is most likely to be C or B♭. Although fully chromatic, playing in the home key gives best results.

So, if you have a Jeffries Duet, congratulations, you are member of a very elite and exclusive club!

Making sense of and getting tunes out of this rare and unusual instrument is the hard part – that's where this book will help. Many have called the keyboard totally "confusing" and "incomprehensible", but there really is a logic to it that allows you to play an amazing variety of tunes and accompaniments.

Just because the Jeffries Duet is fully chromatic that doesn't mean all the notes are easy to find or to get to. Along with simple tunes and chord charts, the tunes in the book are presented in a wide variety of styles with progressive arrangements to show you just what this instrument is capable of.

If you have a Jeffries Duet in a home key other than C, the chords and patterns will still be the same, only the pitch will be different.

The Jeffries Duet Concertina Tutor

HISTORY

The story of the Jeffries Duet begins with a man named Charles Jeffries.

Born in London in 1841 and originally a brushmaker by trade, he began making concertinas in the mid 1860's. Little is known about his shop or his business, but he made some of the finest Anglo concertinas. They are still highly sought-after a hundred years later and can be worth thousands of dollars.

Sometime around the late 1890's he invented the Jeffries Duet system by taking a single row from an Anglo and expanding it into two rows that play the same notes pushing or pulling, and then adding sharps and flats and extra notes around the edges in two additional rows. Many of these duets have distinctive raised metal ends and unique fretwork that is different from his Anglos.

After Charles Jeffries passed away in 1906, his sons continued to make Anglos and Jeffries Duets as the "Jeffries Bros." for another 25 years. Their duets were labeled "Jeffries Bros." (instead of "C. Jeffries") with the address 23 Praed Street, and later 12 Aldershot Road, Kilburn, in London.

The heyday of the Jeffries Duet was in the 1920's, and there are reports of some people converting larger Anglos into Jeffries Duets. C. Wheatstone & Co. built ten "A.G. (Anglo-German) Duets" between 1922 and 1930, and H. Crabb & Son made at least one about that same time and another in 1969. There are no indications that Lachenal & Co. ever made any, but it's possible that one or two might turn up someday.

All totaled, it is estimated that only a few hundred Jeffries Duets were ever made, if that many. This would mean that less than 0.5% of all concertinas made historically were Jeffries Duets – even less than that now considering all the newer concertinas on the market today.

Jeffries never numbered their instruments and they left no known sales records or logs. These are the Jeffries Duets we know of that were built by Wheatstone and Crabb:

C. WHEATSTONE & CO.

#29112	61-button	1922
#30096	48-button	1924
#30374	61-button	1924
#30740	68-button	1925
#30995	46-button	1926
#31850	70-button	1928
#31902	56-button	1928
#32045	53-button	1928
#32286	56-button	1930
#32557	53-button	1930

H. CRABB & SON

No.9055	50-button	1930
No.18298	60-button	1969

THE RAMPIN' CAT

Fast-forward to 1977, when Neil Wayne's Free Reed Records released the first-ever commercial recording featuring the Jeffries Duet concertina.

Titled *The Rampin' Cat*, it showcases the amazing playing of Michael Hebbert on a variety of traditional and British Music Hall favorites on a 50-button Jeffries Duet.

Tracks include "The Star of the County Down", "My Old Dutch", "The Sunny Side of the Street, "The Spaniard That Blighted My Life", "Icicle Joe the Eskimo", "They Wanted a Songbird in Heaven So God Took Caruso Away", and a spectacular rendition of "The Dambusters' March".

Even today this recording is considered to be the gold standard for Jeffries Duet players. It is still available, repackaged on an audio CD with another album from Free Reed Records.

Several tunes from the album are included in this book, and every Jeffries Duet player is encouraged to study and learn (and enjoy) every track.

TRACKLIST

1. Logan Water/Orkney Rope Waltz/Pete's Peerie Boat/Albert's Hornpipe
2. Gathering Codpieces
3. I Do Like To Be Beside The Seaside
4. My Old Dutch
5. Icicle Joe, The Eskimo
6. The Spaniard That Blighted My Life
7. The Quaker's Wife
8. Auld Donald/Merry Month of May/Untitled/Off to Charleston
9. The Sunny Side Of The Street
10. Buddy, Can You Spare A Dime?
11. The Dambusters' March
12. The Indian Queen
13. They Wanted A Songbird In Heaven, So God Took Caruso Away
14. Allan Water
15. Star of the County Down/The American Boot-Dance/Jenny Lind Polka

THE INSTRUMENT

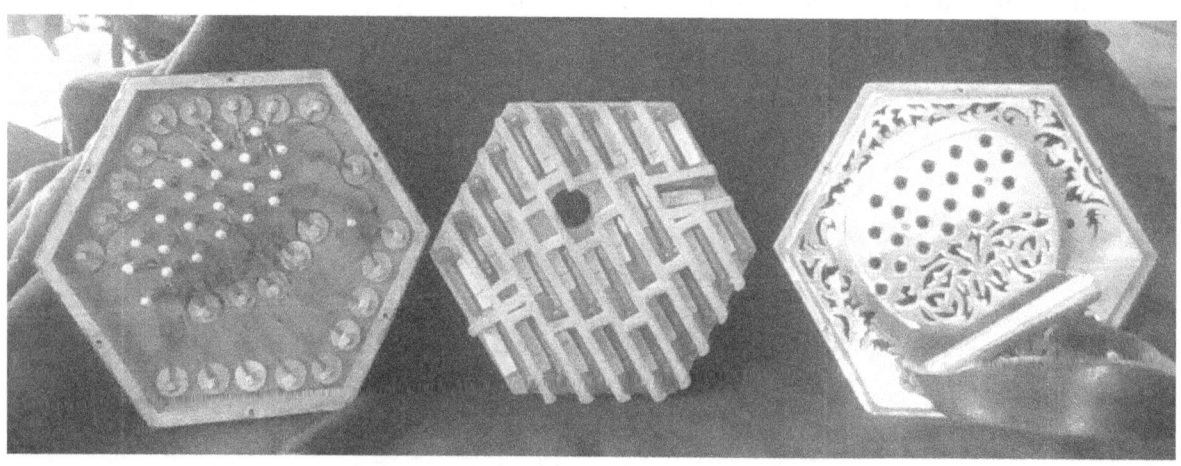
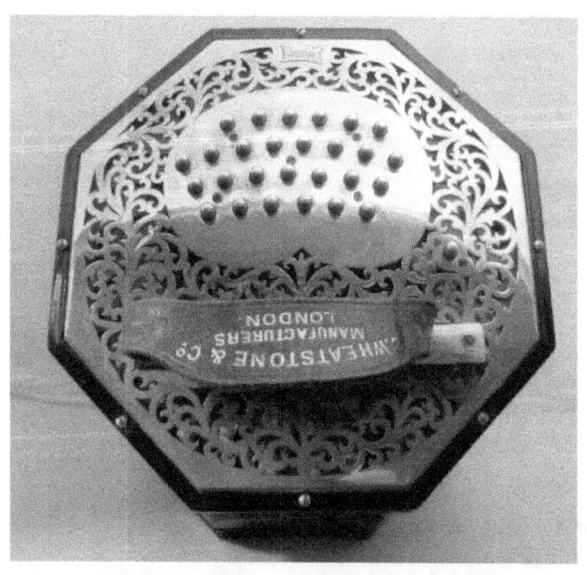

The Jeffries Duet Concertina Tutor

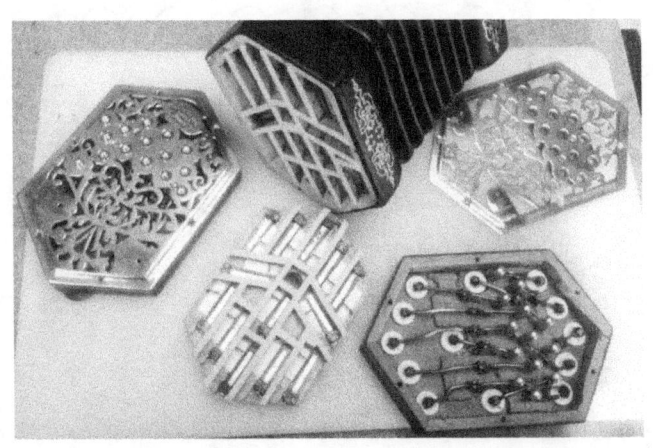
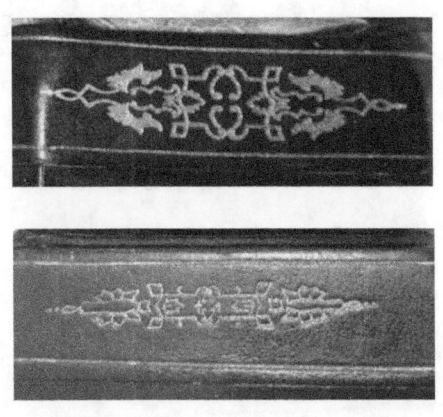

KEYBOARD

The button layout for a 50-button Jeffries Duet in the home key of C looks like this:

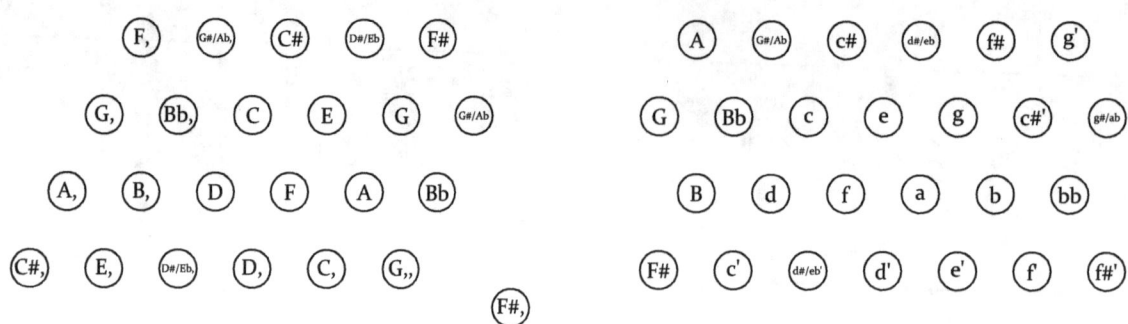

(Note values are shown using abc notation)

Lower notes are on the left, higher notes are on the right, and it is fully chromatic over 3 ½ octaves. Five notes overlap between the two sides. Here's how it compares to a piano keyboard:

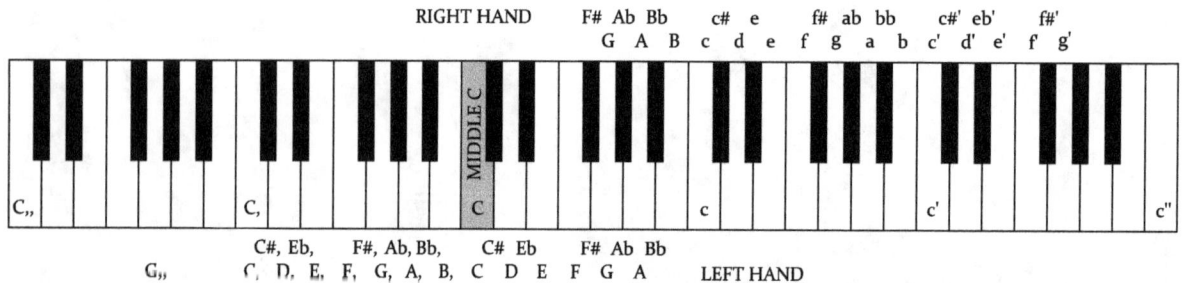

The octave ranges look like this on the layout:

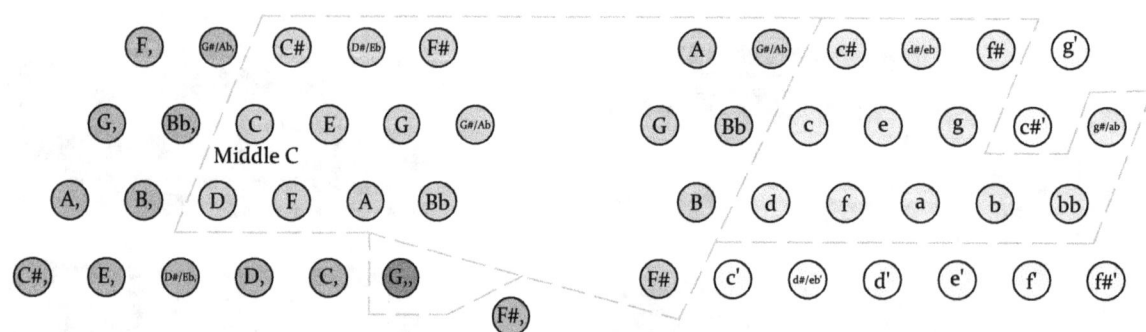

THE HOME KEY

The Jeffries Duet is based on taking one row of an Anglo and expanding it to two rows whose buttons play the same notes of the major scale in either direction of the bellows.

The key of these expanded major scale rows is referred to as the "home key" of the instrument. This major scale is a sawtooth pattern in the middle two rows on each side. The "C" in the middle of the left side corresponds to middle C on the piano.

Play "C" on the left side with your ring finger, and "c" on the right with your middle finger.

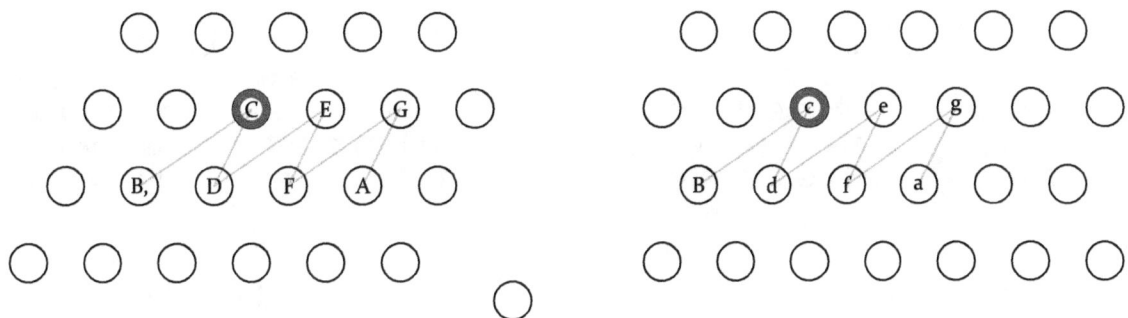

The sawtooth pattern only works for these seven notes of the major scale on each side. Extending the C major scale up or down looks like this:

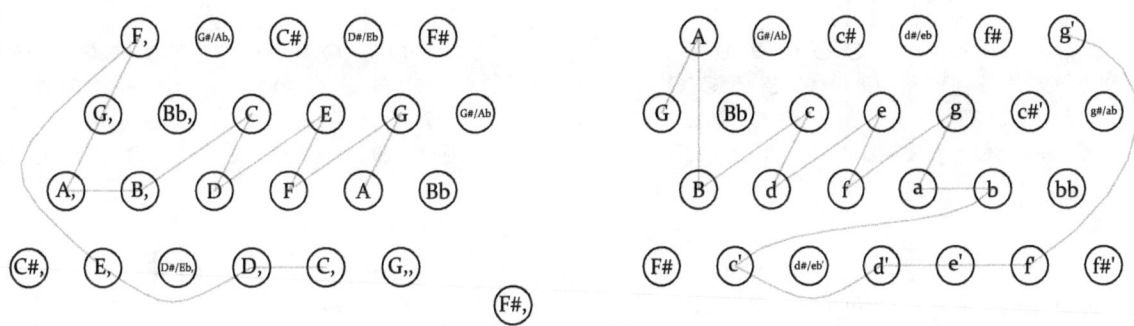

Although the Jeffries Duet is fully chromatic through 3 ½ octaves, you will find the home key is by far and away the easiest key to play in. The home key will typically be C or B♭, but other instruments might have home keys of F, G, A, A♭, or D.

Playing in keys outside the home key usually involves a significant amount of daring and dexterity.

Scales in other keys become a lot more problematical, and this is probably the main reason why many people have found the Jeffries Duet to be anywhere from "difficult" to "incomprehensible".

Here are the patterns for the major scales in all the other keys:

C F#/Gb

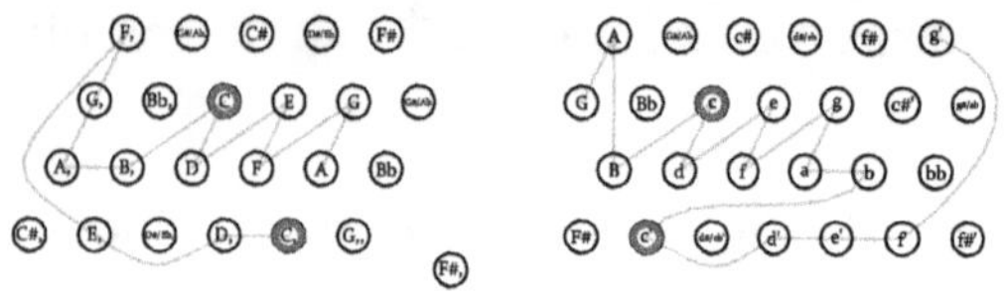

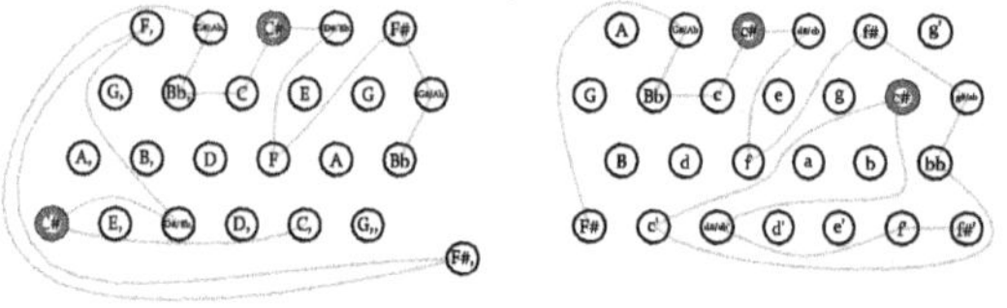

C#/Db G

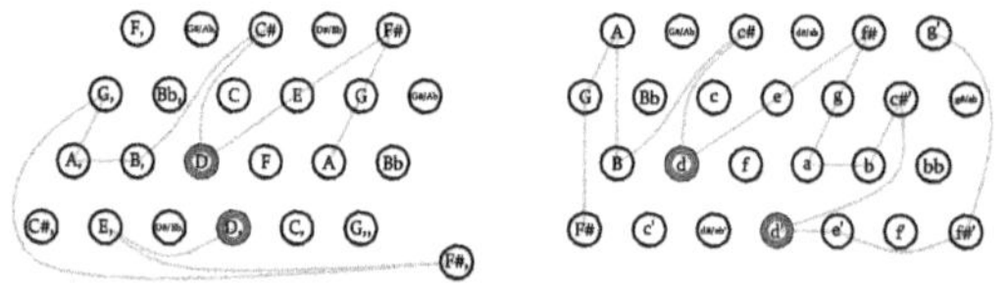

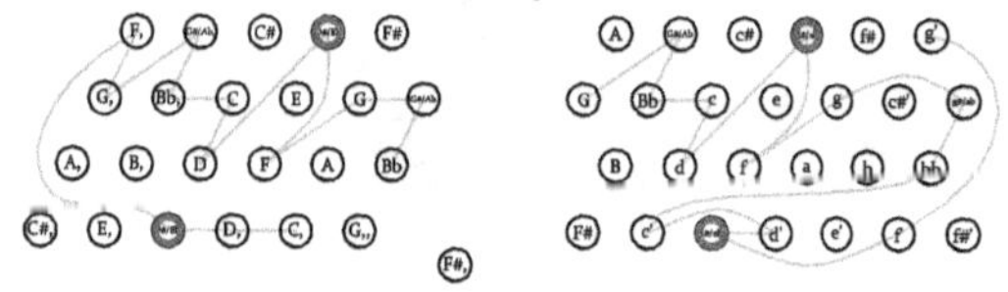

D G#/Ab

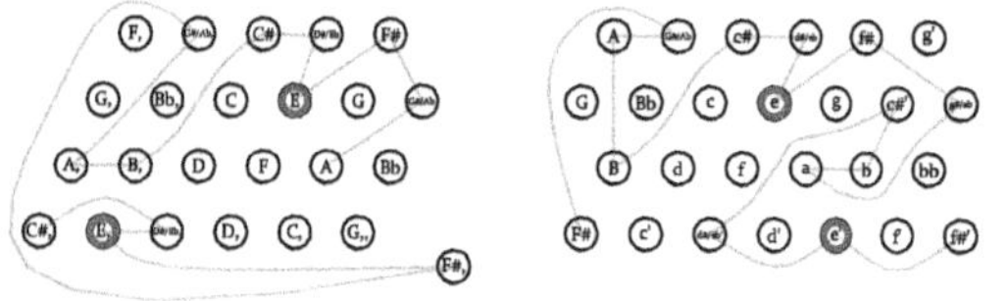

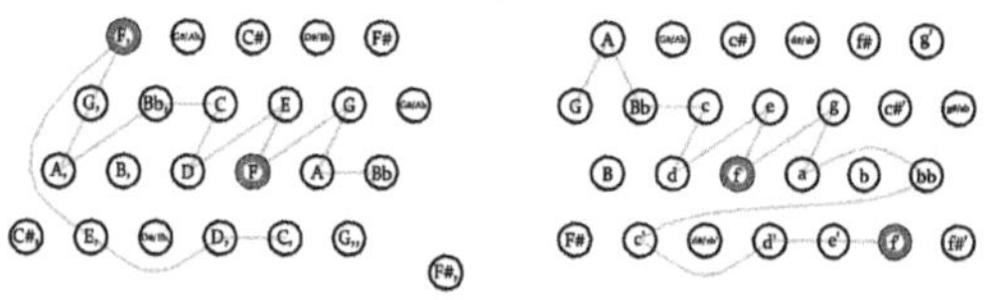

D#/Eb A

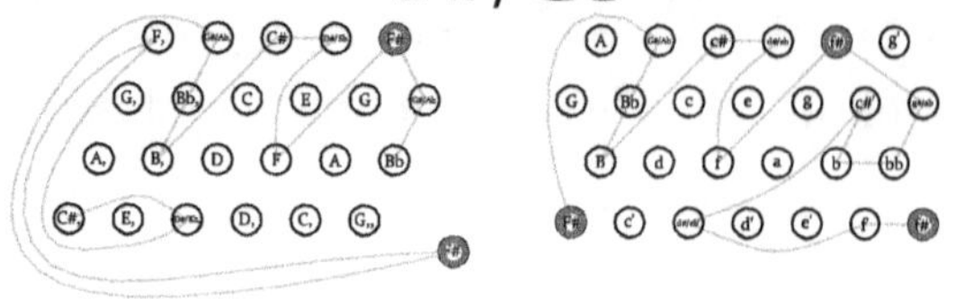

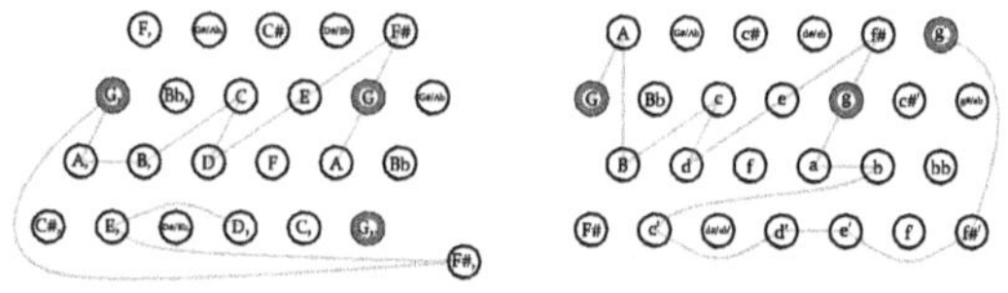

E A#/Bb

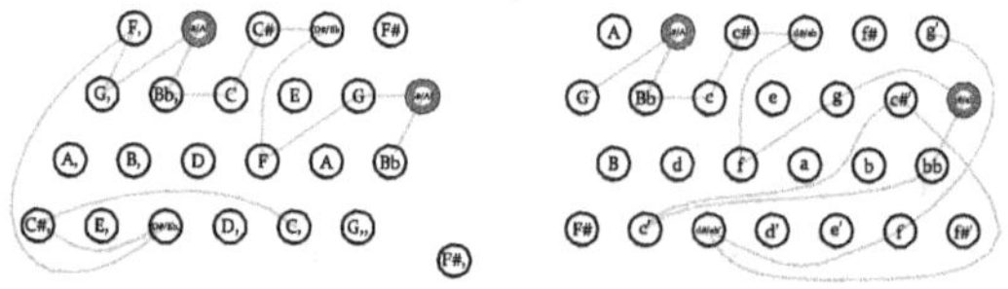

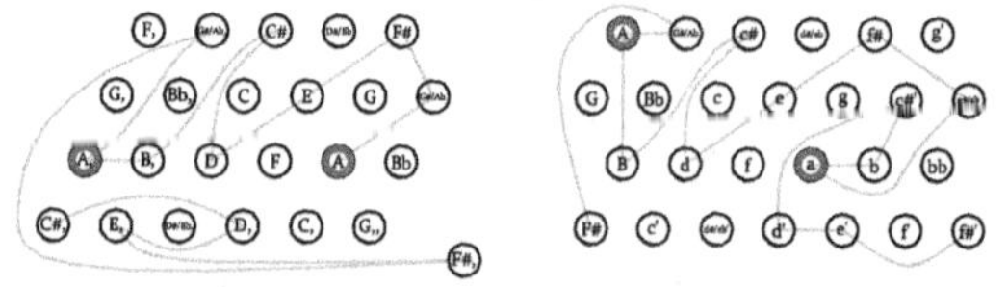

F B

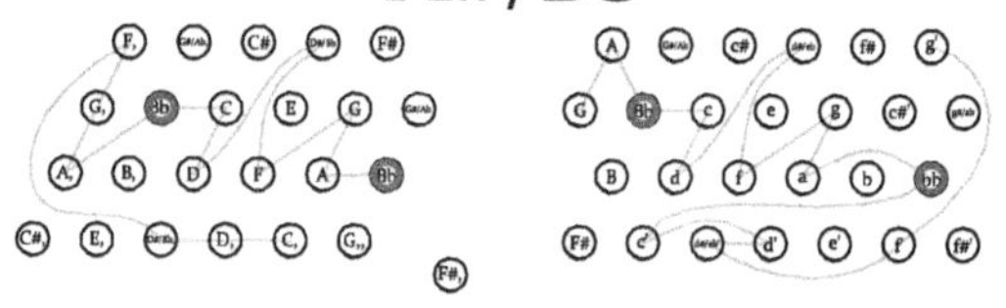

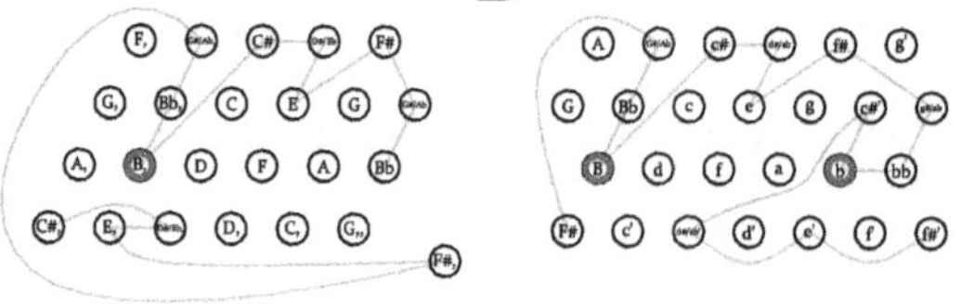

PATTERNS

The note patterns are not consistent between the two sides, but here are the areas that are, along with the five notes that overlap:

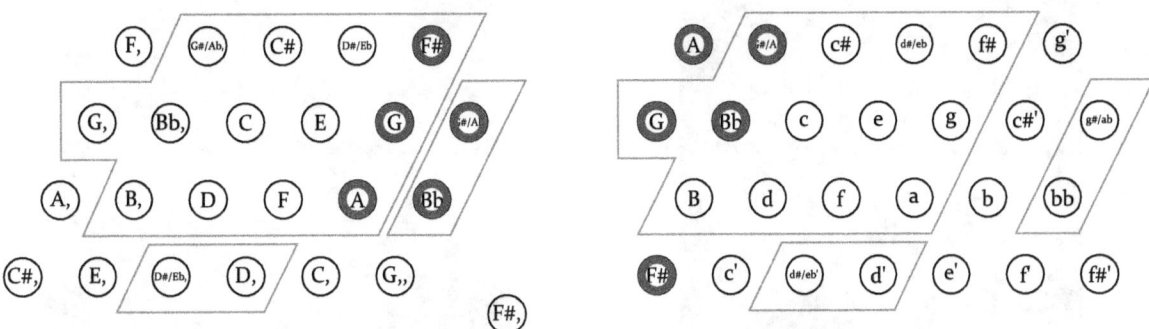

Finding sharps and flats from the home key "core" is something that just needs to be learned, but as you can see, the most common sharps and flats are close by and easy to get to.

SHARPS

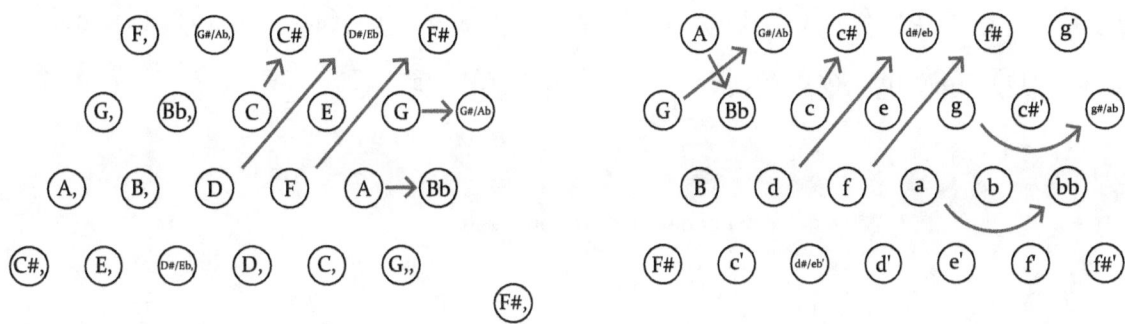

FLATS

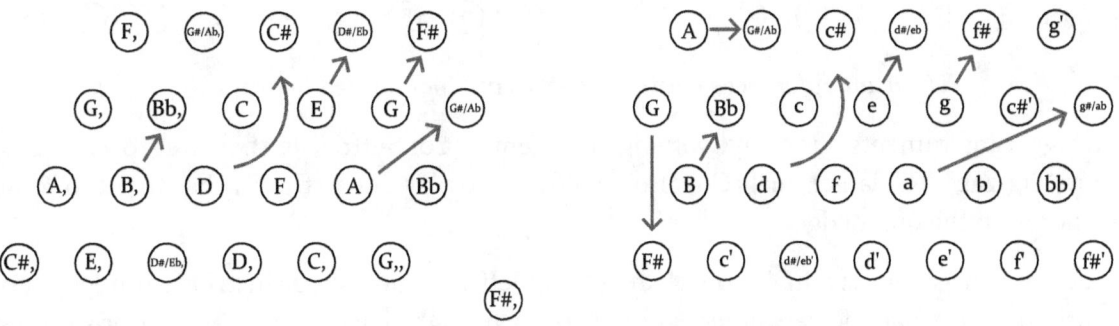

LARGER INSTRUMENTS

Larger instruments with 60+ button keyboards can look like this:

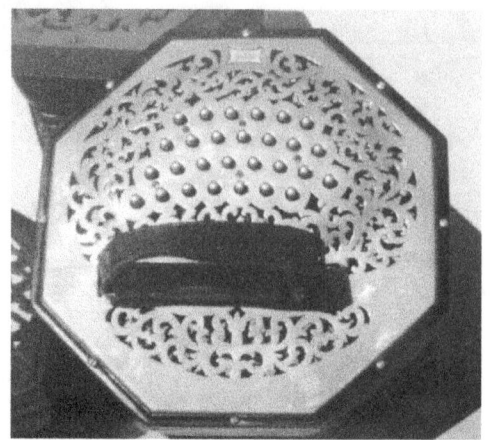

JEFFRIES 62-BUTTON

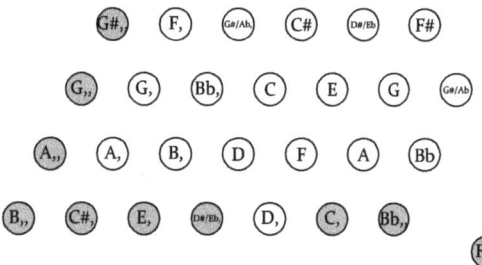
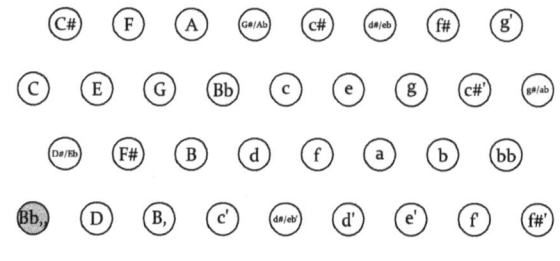

WHEATSTONE 61-BUTTON - #29112

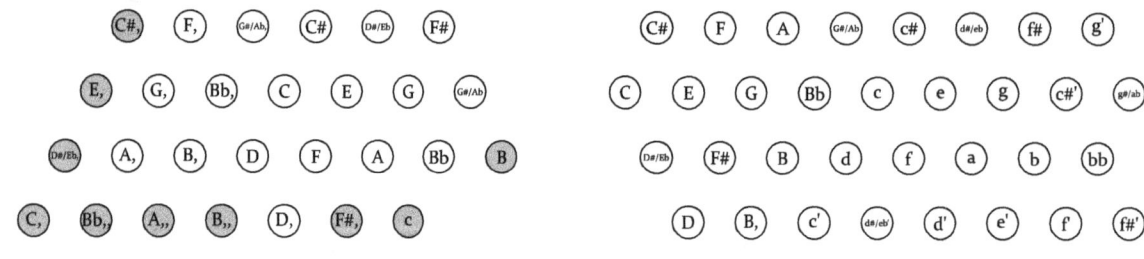

(button differences between the two are highlighted in gray)

These bigger instruments often have varying arrangements of buttons in the outer rows outside the core "zig-zag". The larger duets can also be difficult to play due to the reaches to get to some of the notes on the outer edges.

This lack of consistency is a major problem with all Jeffries Duets. Your instrument might vary from others, and what you've worked so hard to learn might have some major surprises on a different Jeffries Duet.

Hopefully the 50-button layout in this book will be similar to your instrument. If not, simply adapt and overcome as necessary. A large keyboard map for a 50-button instrument in the home key of C is in the back of the book for you to cut out and keep handy while you learn the notes.

TABLATURE

Because there can be so much variation in the locations of particular notes outside the core pattern, the buttons are indicated by showing note values instead of specific button numbers.

All of the tunes are shown with the melody in standard musical notation, and with the pitches of all notes and accompaniments shown in "abc notation".

How the tablature works in this book:

- The buttons are identified using "abc notation" to indicate pitch.
- Buttons on the right-hand side are shown above the musical notes.
- Buttons on the left-hand side are shown below the musical notes.
- For chords, the lower pitches are shown at the bottom of the vertical stack and the higher pitches are at the top.
- Notes that are held for a longer period of time are indicated with dashed lines after the button number.
- Chord symbols are shown along the top of each line of music.

EXAMPLE:

Every tune also has a Button Map showing which buttons are needed for that particular tune:

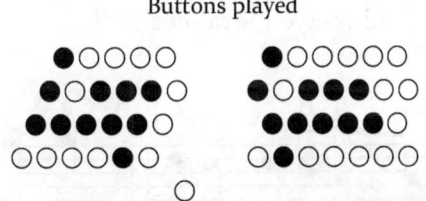

The Jeffries Duet Concertina Tutor

RIGHT HAND MELODY

For tunes in the home key, "Twinkle Twinkle Little Star" is a good example that uses the basic core, or sawtooth, pattern:

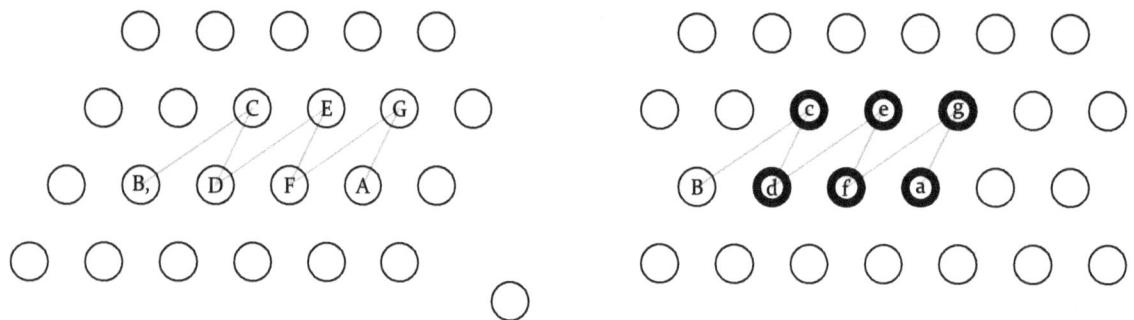

"Twinkle Twinkle Little Star" notation looks like this for the melody on the right-hand side:

You can also play these same notes an octave lower on the left-hand side since the pattern is identical. If you put the right hand and left hand together you'll be playing in octaves.

You'll find that many melodies will also use these three notes to the left:

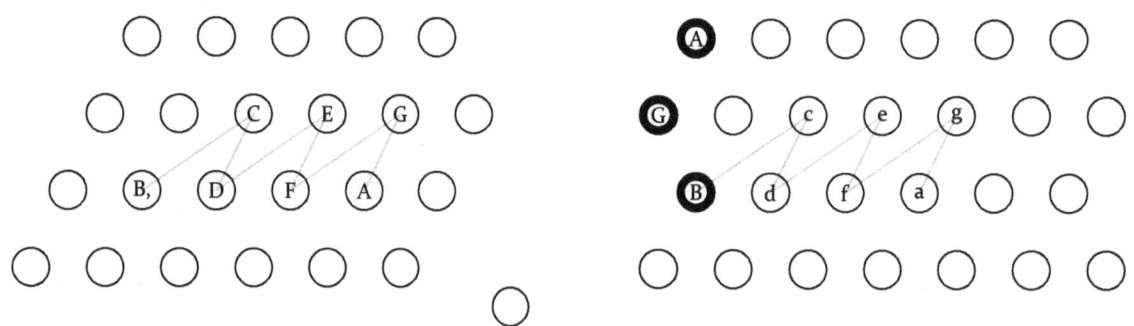

Here's an example from the tune "Blue-Eyed Stranger":

If you want to play this melody on the left hand or in octaves, you'll run into the first major inconsistency of the Jeffries Duet button layout.

For this tune, the pattern on both sides is identical except for one major exception. Most instruments will have the octave A note in different places on the right and left sides:

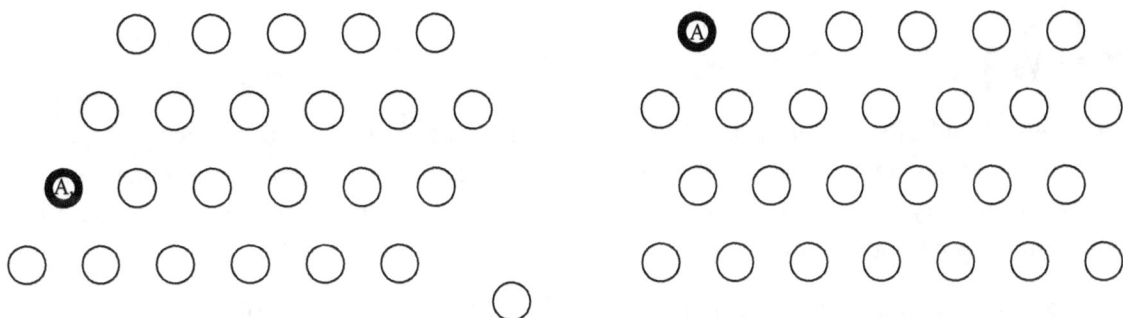

As you can see, it's up high on the right-hand side, but down low on the left-hand side, and playing both in octaves will take some getting used to.

A lot of melodies will also go higher than the core sawtooth, and will most commonly use these four notes:

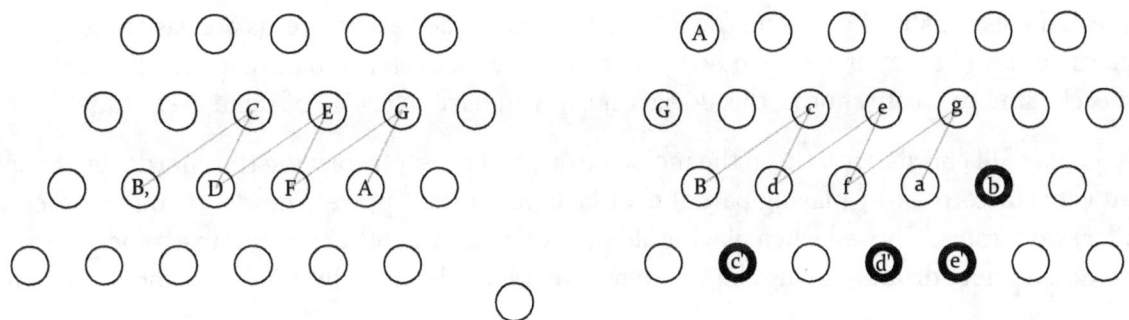

Here's an example from "The Mudgee Waltz":

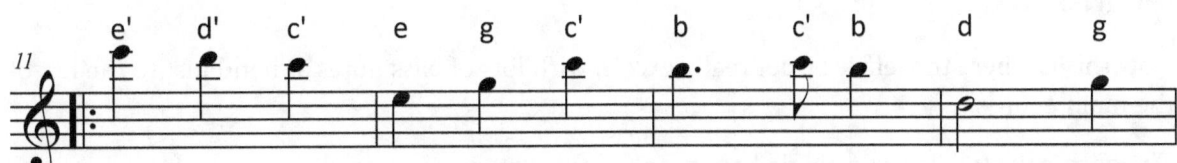

Once you start playing more and more tunes outside the central sawtooth (B-c-d-e-f-g-a) and the adjoining four accidentals on the top row (G#/A♭-c#-d#/e♭-f#) you will be constantly confronted with octave notes located in different places between the two sides.

ACCOMPANIMENT TECHNIQUES

The full power of the Jeffries Duet is in its ready ability to play an impressive variety of song and tune accompaniments, especially if you are playing in the home key. Melody on the right and accompaniment on the left is the most common, but your options are wide open and fully chromatic on both sides. Feel free to experiment and find notes and unusual chords.

OCTAVES

A great way to add extra emphasis and volume, but it can get really tricky once you get out of the central zigzag since the patterns outside the sawtooth on both sides are not consistent. Fear not, motor memory will eventually make light work of the finger patterns even if they are initially challenging. It's a great sound that just has to be learned and practiced.

Octaves on the right side only are particularly difficult but can add a lot of emphasis.

SIMPLE HARMONIES

If you want to play single-note harmonies, you have the entire left side keyboard to choose from, and can play in thirds, or fifths, or whatever notes sound good to you. You can also include harmony notes on the right-hand side.

CHORDS

Chords are especially effective on the Jeffries Duet, and the basic patterns are easy to learn, but you can easily overpower the melody if you're not careful. Even if you have four fingers available on each hand to create chords, this doesn't mean you have to use all of them every time.

If you play full chords, try to keep the melody front and center by playing the chords very crisply and very staccato, or by playing partial chords. Open fifths ("power chords" if you're a rock-n-roller) work especially well when playing alongside fiddles and other musical instruments. Single and double-note drones can also be very effective. Make the melody stand out, don't drown it.

You can also break the chords up into arpeggios by playing each note of the chord separately one after the other, either up or down the scale.

OOM-PAH

Now this is where the Jeffries Duet really excels, with lots of bass notes at hand just to the left of the main chords.

The oom-pah style is just a single bass note followed by one or two chords, simple as that. The emphasis is on the downbeat played on the bass note. Tapping the chords lightly gives a much a crisper sound.

And get ready – your left-hand pinkie finger will get quite the workout. It may be really hard to train at first, but persevere and you'll be able to play all sorts of interesting bass note accompaniments, runs, and walk-downs.

In the home key, you'll use these bass notes to the left of the zigzag most often for oompah accompaniment:

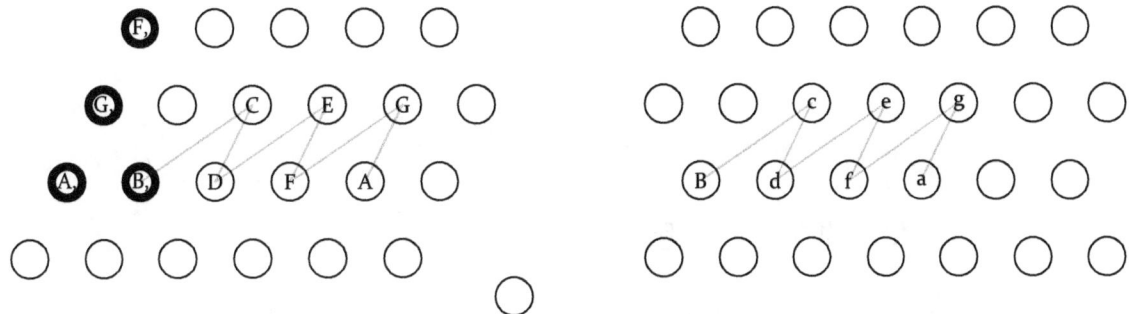

Here's an example from the tune, "Portsmouth":

A variation on the oom-pah style is to add a bass "walkdown" like this from "Galopede":

LEFT HAND MELODY

Another accompaniment variation that works well on the Jeffries Duet is to play the melody on the left hand while tapping chords lightly on the right. Here's an example from "They Needed A Songbird In Heaven So God Took Caruso Away":

LEFT HAND CHORDS

In the home key of C, practice playing and recognizing these chord patterns and notations:

C

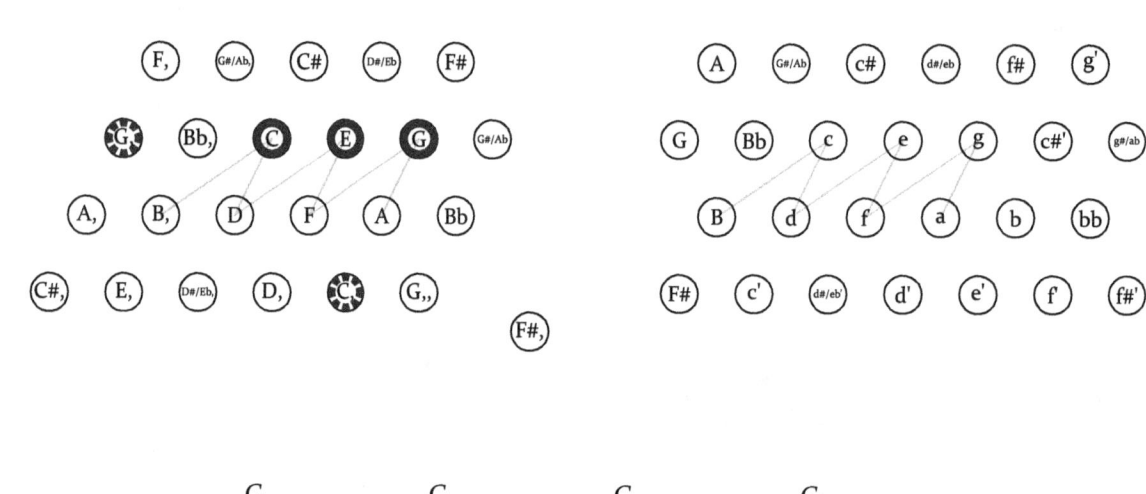

```
        G       G       G       G
        E       E       E       E
        C       C       C       C
C           G,      C           G,      C,
```

F

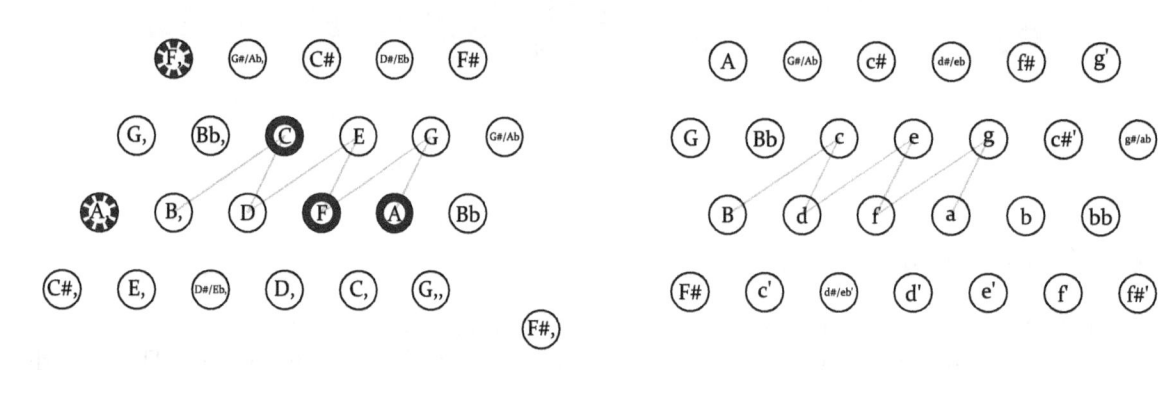

```
        A       A       A       A
        F       F       F       F
        C       C       C       C
F,          A,      F,          A,      F,
```

G

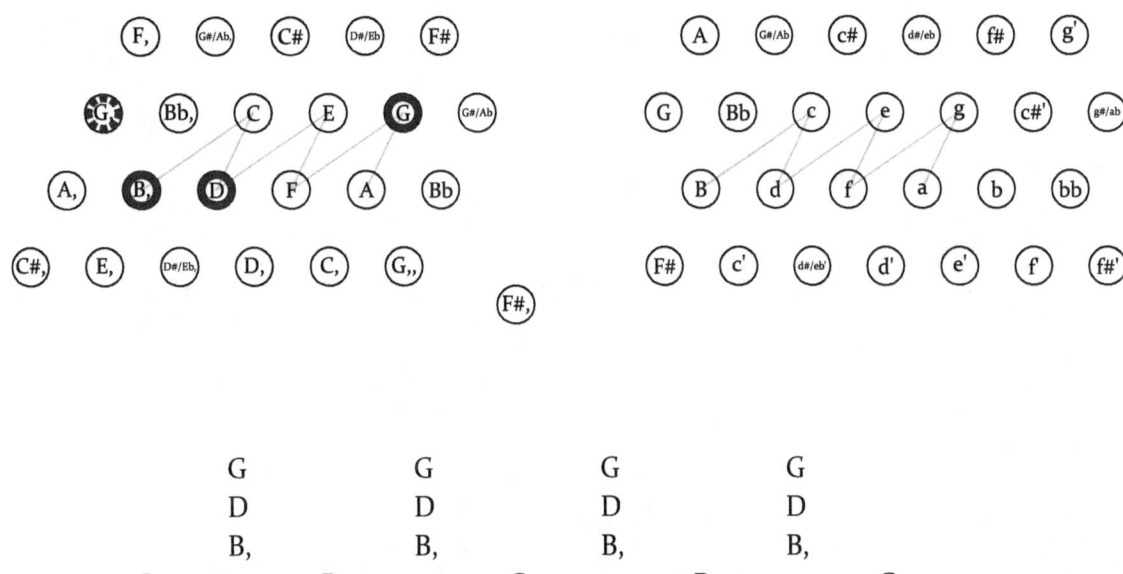

Am

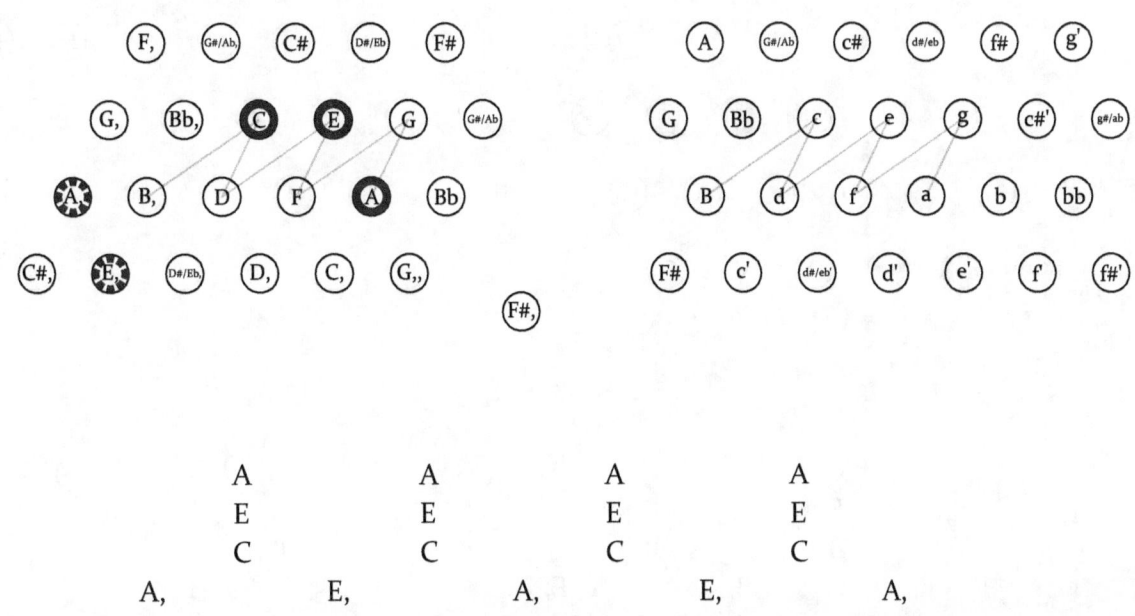

D

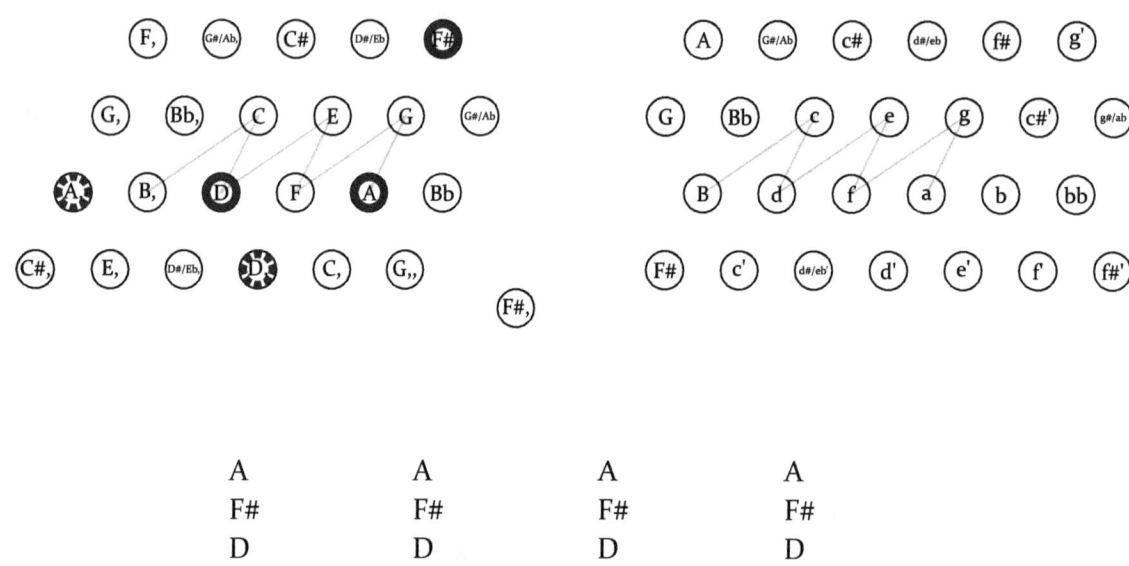

```
            A           A           A           A
            F#          F#          F#          F#
            D           D           D           D
D                A,          D           A,          D,
```

Em

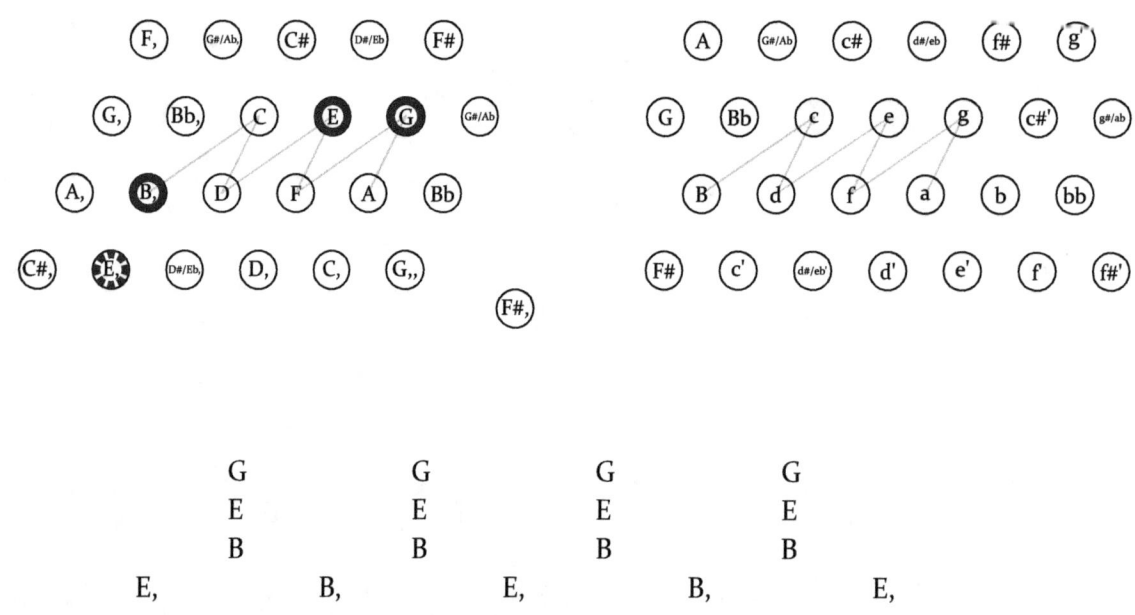

```
            G           G           G           G
            E           E           E           E
            B           B           B           B
E,               B,          E,          B,          E,
```

A

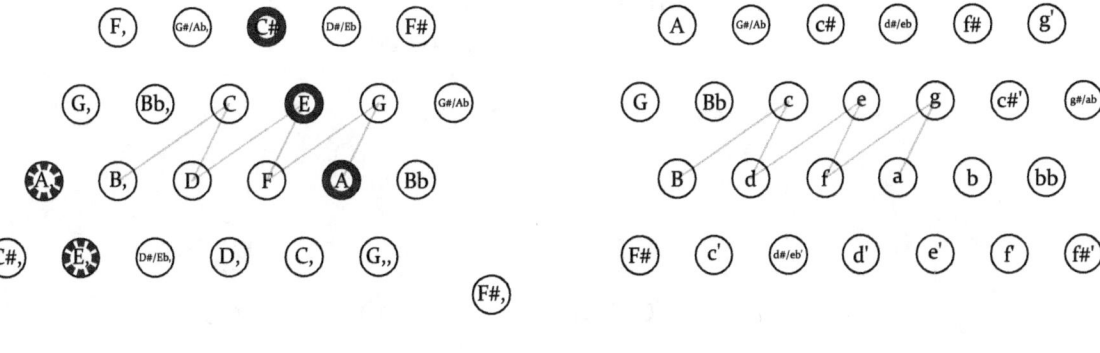

	A	A	A	A
	E	E	E	E
	C#	C#	C#	C#
A,		E,		A,		E,		A,

Dm

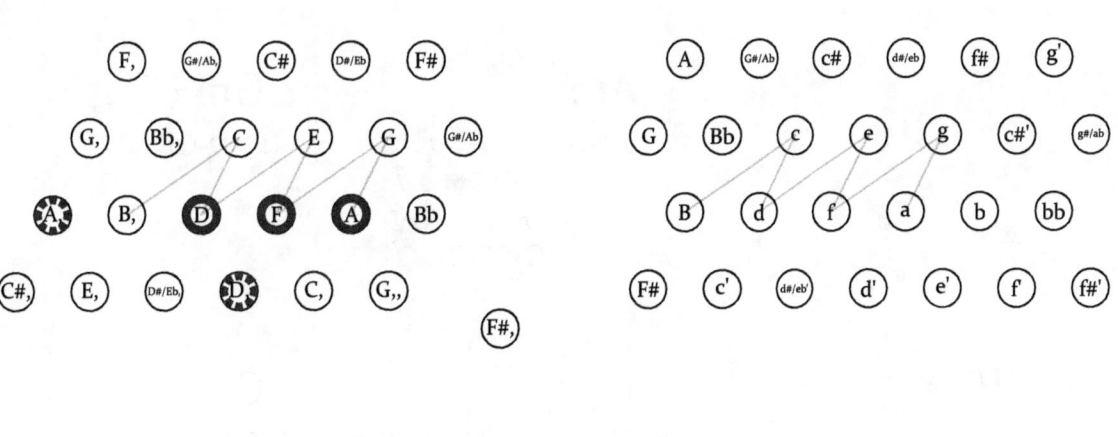

	A	A	A	A
	F	F	F	F
	D	D	D	D
D		A,		D		A,		D

The Jeffries Duet Concertina Tutor

Common Left-Hand Chords
[including lowest bass note and 7th]

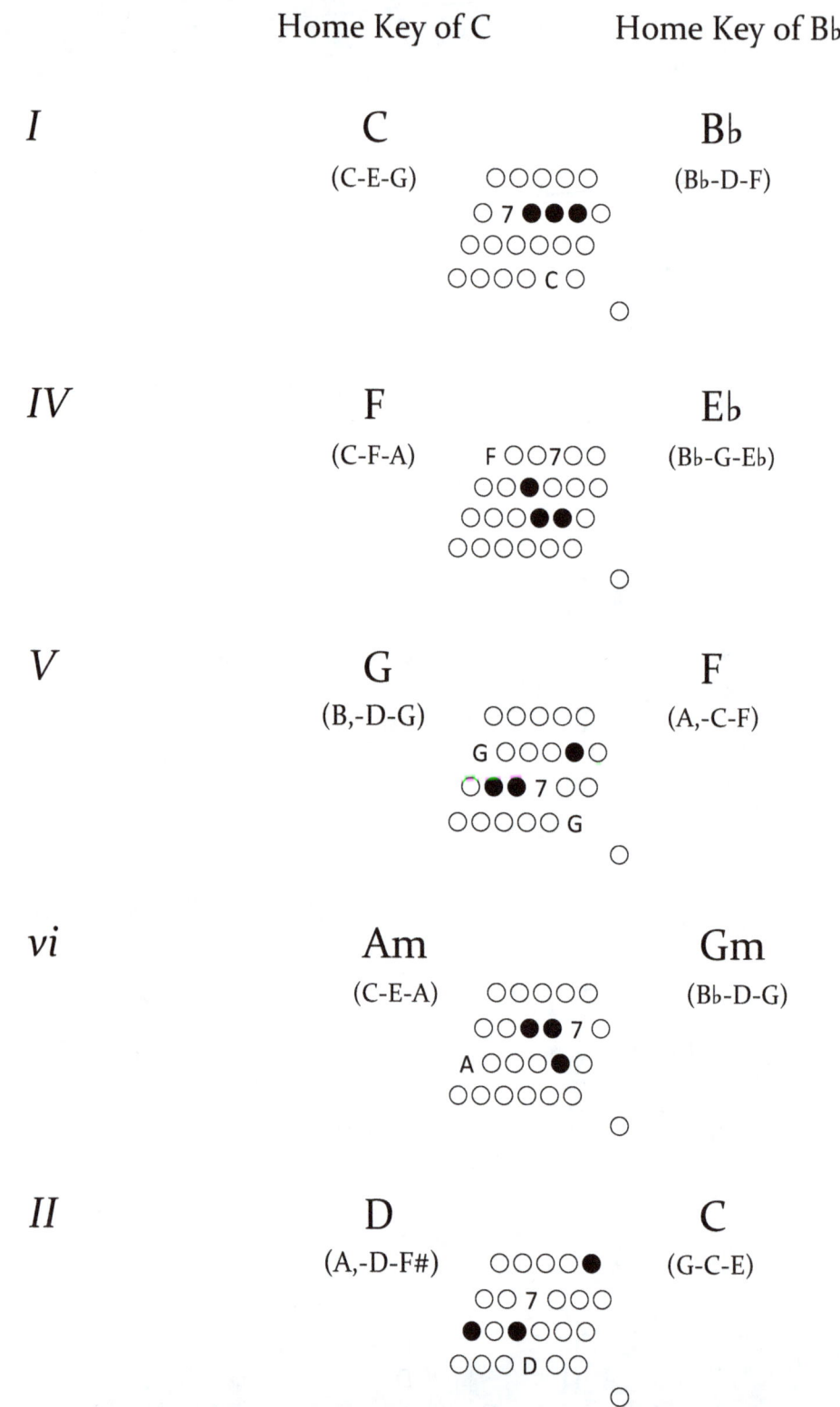

Home Key of C   Home Key of B♭

III **E** **D**
(B,-E-G#) (A-D-F#)

VI **A** **G**
(C#-E-A) (B-D-G)

VII♭ **B♭** **A♭**
(B♭-D-F) (A♭-C-E♭)

ii **Dm** **Cm**
(D-F-A) (C-E♭-G)

iii **Em** **Dm**
(B-E-G) (A-D-F)

vii **Bm** **Am**
(B-D-F#) (A-C-E)

The Jeffries Duet Concertina Tutor

Complex Chords

Using the C-chord as an example, here are some of the more colorful and complex left-hand chords:

C major
C-E-G

C minor
C-E♭-G

C7 (dominant)
C-E-G-B♭

Cmaj7
C-E-G-B

Cmaj7+5
C-E-G#-B

Cmaj7-5
C-E-F#-B

C+ (augmented)
C-E-G#

C° or Cdim
C-E♭-F#-A

Cm7-5
C-E♭-F#-B♭

Csus4
C-F-G

Combining both hands and chords into one graphic:

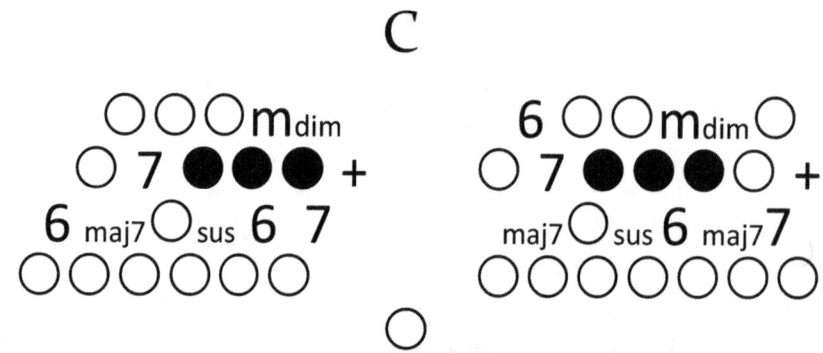

PLAYING IN DIFFERENT KEYS

The Jeffries Duet is designed to work best in the home key, and most of the notes will be in the central zigzag pattern plus a few easily-reachable notes along the edges.

Transposing music to a key that better suits your instrument is something you will probably do fairly often. Perfectly ok if you are only playing by yourself, but if you want to play with others then you will need to play in the original key or the key that they are playing in.

You'll find the level of difficulty varies greatly from key to key on the Jeffries Duet. Some notes will be easy to find and reach while others will be less logical and a bit of a challenge. The key of F often works well on a C instrument, other keys are a little trickier. When playing in the keys of G and D on a C instrument, the higher F# notes are adjacent to the G notes and will be difficult to reach if the tune calls for F# and E or G to be played in sequence.

Here is the first part of "Twinkle Twinkle Little Star" in six different keys:

The Jeffries Duet Concertina Tutor

WHAT IF MY DUET IS IN A DIFFERENT HOME KEY?

This book is written for a 50-button Jeffries Duet in the home key of C. Instruments were also made in other home keys: B♭ appears to be the most prevalent – F, A, A♭, G and D have also been reported. Many were originally in old high pitch (A=452 Hz instead of the current modern pitch of A=440 Hz), so you may find one that has been retuned up or down from its original key.

If your instrument is not in C, you have two choices:

1. Ignore the difference in pitch and play it as if it were in the key of C.

    This is the easiest solution, but works if you only intend to play by yourself and are not concerned about the difference between written and sounding pitch. This will allow you to learn all the tunes and chord patterns in this book without having to make any changes.

2. Learn the buttons and notes in real pitch.

    If you intend to play with others, or read directly from music, or play in many different keys, then you will need to learn actual pitches and buttons. It's a lot of work, but you can transpose the music in this book to the key that works with your instrument by penciling in the new notes. Since you'll be out of the home key, you might end up with some unusual reaches and stretches to get the notes you want.

Either way, it is highly recommended that you invest in a program like *The Amazing Slow Downer*® (www.ronimusic.com) or *Audacity* (www.audacityteam.org) so you can freely change the pitches of existing recordings to match your instrument while you are learning.

...OR HAS LOTS MORE BUTTONS?

First thing, make a button map!

And then figure out the pitch and octave of each and every note.

Study it and learn where the extra buttons are and have fun experimenting with how they can best be used for additional notes, chords and accompaniments.

The extra buttons usually provide additional overlapping notes between the two sides plus more bass notes in the lower end. For some of the larger instruments the lower buttons can be very difficult to reach.

Just don't expect much consistency if you're moving between instruments of different sizes, as larger Jeffries Duets vary from instrument to instrument. The basic sawtooth pattern will be the same, but most of the differences will be in the notes around the edges, especially in the lower bass notes.

ANGLO VS JEFFRIES DUET

- Both look a lot alike, with handstraps and horizontal rows of buttons on each side, with lower notes on the left and higher notes on the right.

- The "Anglo-German" concertina ("Anglo") is the most popular concertina system and has been in continuous production worldwide since its invention in the 1830's, while the Jeffries Duet is incredibly scarce.

- New English and Anglo concertinas are readily available from a wide variety of shops and manufacturers; there are no new Jeffries Duets – the last one was made over 50 years ago. It is a testament to the high quality of Jeffries construction that so many have survived to the present and are often still in top working order.

- Some Jeffries Anglos might have started out as Jeffries Duets but were converted due to the higher demand for Anglos and the legendary high quality of Jeffries reeds. It is most unfortunate that many duets over the years were converted or cannibalized because someone found them too difficult to play – hopefully this book will reverse that trend. In addition to the loss of a rare and valuable duet, conversion typically results in overly heavy Anglos with too many buttons in non-standard layouts.

- The second row (home key) of the Jeffries Duet is essentially the same as pushing the top row of the 20-button Anglo or the middle row of a 30-button Anglo.

- The left-hand "C" finger position is virtually identical to that of the Anglo, but on the right-hand side the "c" is played with the middle finger instead of the index finger.

- The 30-button Anglo has accidentals on the top row, so too does the Jeffries Duet, but they are in different places.

- The Anglo chord patterns are exactly the same for the C chord, but slightly different for all the others. Different enough that it can really trip you up if you're switching between the two instruments.

- The low F and low A on the left side are in the same place for both Anglo and Jeffries Duet, but the corresponding chord patterns are different.

- If you play lots of bass notes and chords on the Anglo, they will be mostly in different places on the Jeffries Duet.

- You can play much more complex chords on the Jeffries Duet than you can on the Anglo.

- Last, but not least, do not try to play the same tunes on the Anglo *and* the Jeffries Duet, or you will be asking for a world of trouble, with the end result likely being the inability to play those same tunes on either instrument!

WHAT OTHER JEFFRIES DUET PLAYERS SAY

MICHAEL HEBBERT

"I have learned and always played it intuitively. The more I try to concentrate on what I'm doing, the more wrong notes I hit."

"However, from having run various duet workshops I would be inclined to use the left hand for bass line and countermelody (or melody in octaves) rather than chords. Full chordal harmonies come out too loud on a concertina."

"So for a tune like 'Galopede' the crucial thing for a beginner is to locate those bottom C, G and F buttons and punch them in on the first and third beat of the bar. Get the oom right and the pah can come later."

"The left hand can carry a melody, also learn how to do a staccato left if accompanying a legato right-hand melody."

STUART ESTELL

"The Jeffries system, or the 'demented typewriter' as I like to call it, is a peculiar beast - and has a character all of its own. On paper the layout admittedly does look crackers; regardless of its back-of-fag-packet 'let's reuse anglo end plates' origins, I find it much more manageable than the Maccann keyboard in remoter keys. The Maccann makes me think, the Jeffries just lets me play."

GAVIN ATKIN

"Figure out the arithmetic of the chords, then identify inversions that you can physically play and which sound good. These are skills you have to develop."

"Material for classical guitar sometimes works well on the Jeffries."

"Right hand octaves? If you haven't done so, it's worth the time getting your octave scales down when you can. There's no need to do it everywhere - just here and there where it seems to help the 'call and response' of the phrasing."

ERIK HOUSE

"I usually favor the left hand right up to the end of the overlap zone when I can and use the right for grace notes and escaping fingering difficulties. This comes from fiddle, guitar and banjo where the left is the noting hand but also because my ear prefers the lower range. In fact I've taken to playing the viola for dances when we have another fiddler and the 50 button JD covers the range of both, plus that low G! No need to try to cram every tune onto the right-hand side."

HIDETOSHI YAMASHITA

"I think when I use chords in many cases, only the root of the chord can be suitable for accompaniment than 2 or 3 notes of the chord."

NICK ROBERTSHAW

"Simply decide which notes you want to play and in what order and press the buttons accordingly (accordionly?)"

TUNES

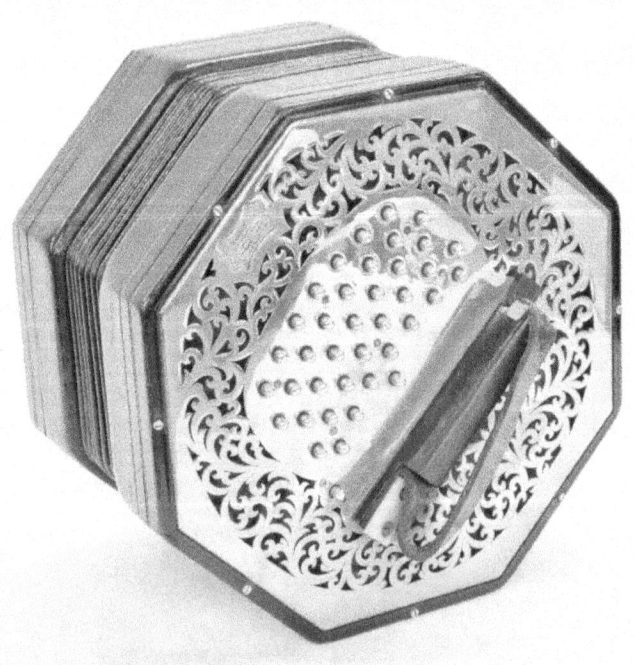

One of America's most famous nursery rhymes, with music written by Lowell Mason in 1830. This will introduce you to the top three notes of the sawtooth pattern in the key of C. You can also play it on the left side since the pattern is identical.

Mary Had a Little Lamb

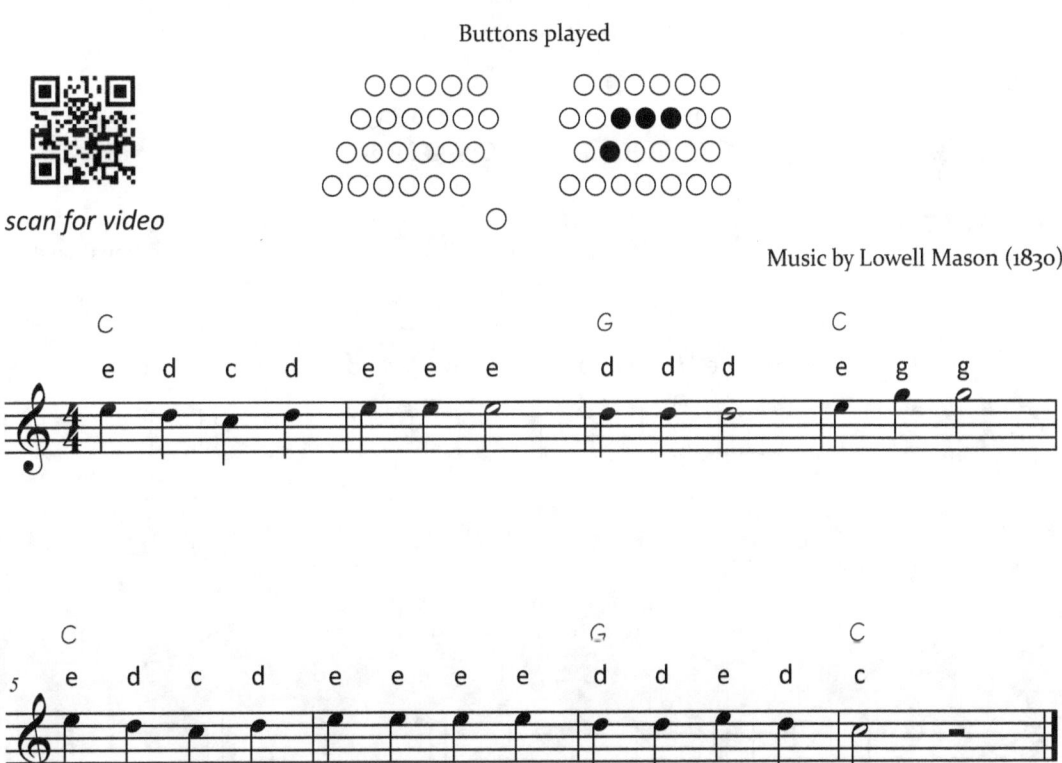

Music by Lowell Mason (1830)

This is the tune of a traditional sea shanty that can be played on only four notes of the right-hand sawtooth zigzag, starting with "c" (use your middle finger). The same pattern is on the left side, and you can play both sides together to play in octaves.

Poor Old Horse (C)

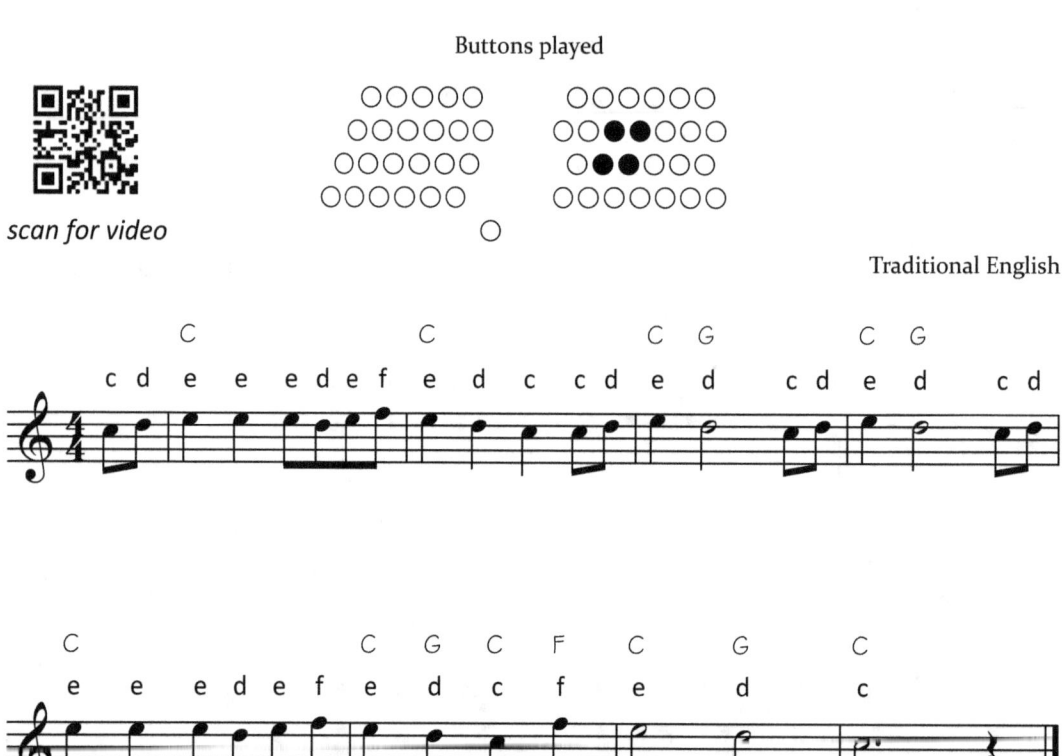

Traditional English

The same tune in the key of G gives you a good introduction to the three notes below c on the right-hand side.

Poor Old Horse (G)

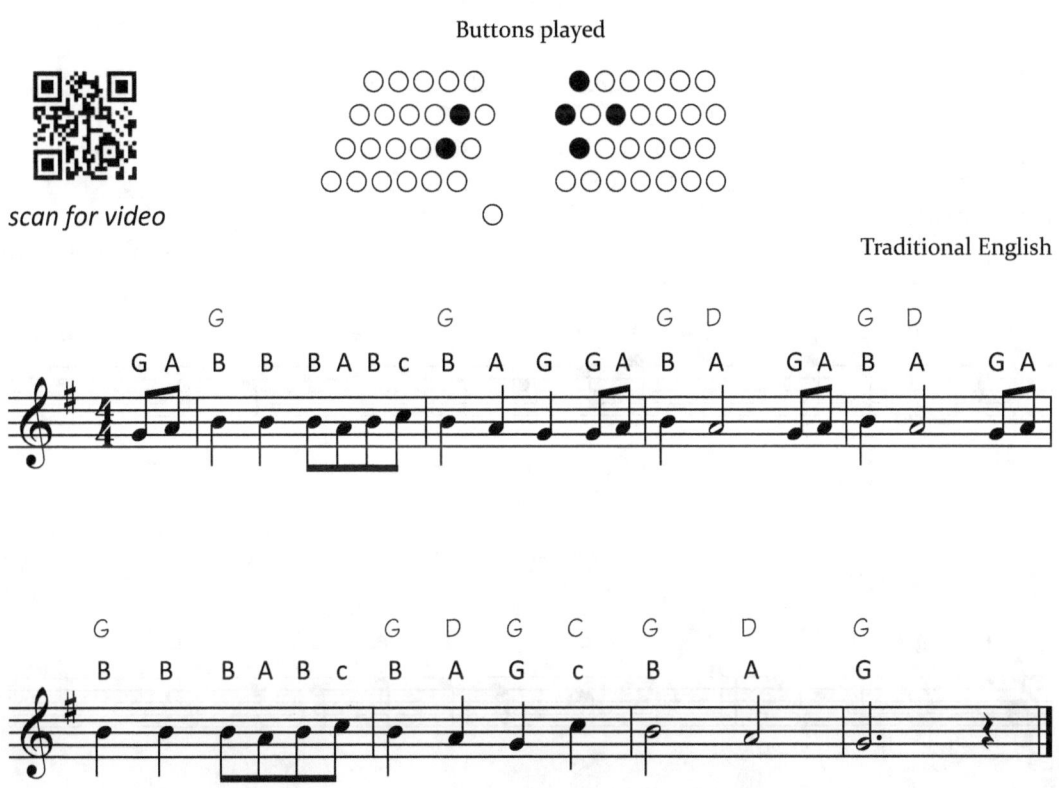

You can also play it "across the break" using buttons on both sides:

The Jeffries Duet Concertina Tutor

This Stephen Foster tune uses six of the notes in the core zigzag. You can also try to play it on the left-hand side, and then together in octaves.

Oh Susanna

Buttons played

scan for video

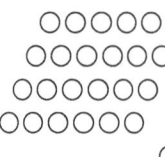 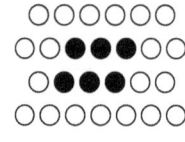

Stephen Foster (1848)

A

B

Another familiar tune that can be played on six notes of the right-hand core pattern, and it can also be played with the exact same pattern on the left-hand side.

Twinkle Twinkle Little Star

Buttons played

scan for video

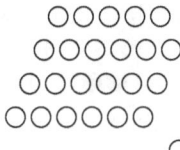
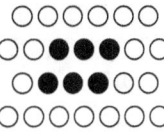

Traditional French, c.1761

A
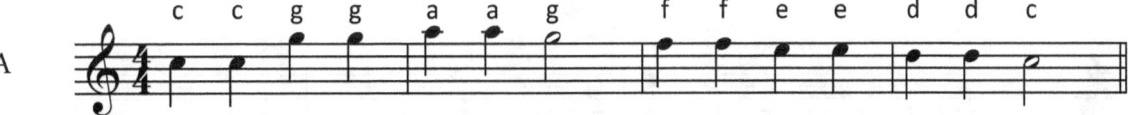

B
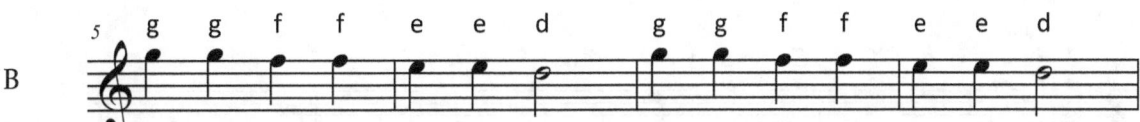

This traditional French tune is played on six notes of the right-hand core zigzag plus the low G.

Frere Jacques

Buttons played

scan for video

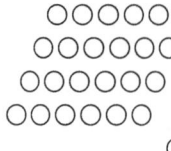 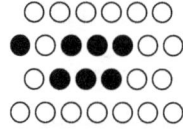

Traditional French

A traditional English dance tune, the words of which became quite the pop culture rage in the 1850's and might have something to with spinning, or more probably, pawning a coat for food and drink. Another good exercise for working the right-hand zigzag and adding the lower G.

Pop Goes the Weasel

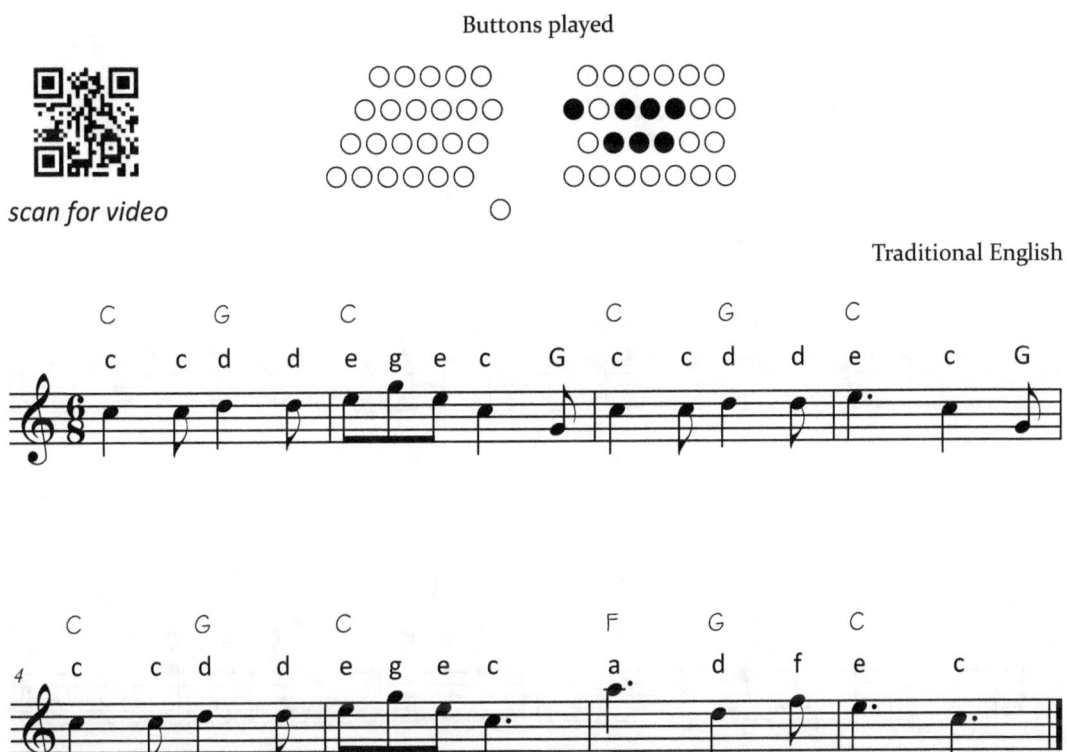

Traditional English

A simple tune that only needs five buttons on the right, and showing various ways to add simple accompaniments on the left. Feel free to experiment and try other chords and variations. And yes, that weird chord in the fourth variation is deliberate – to inspire you to try other options.

Variations on Shepherd's Hey

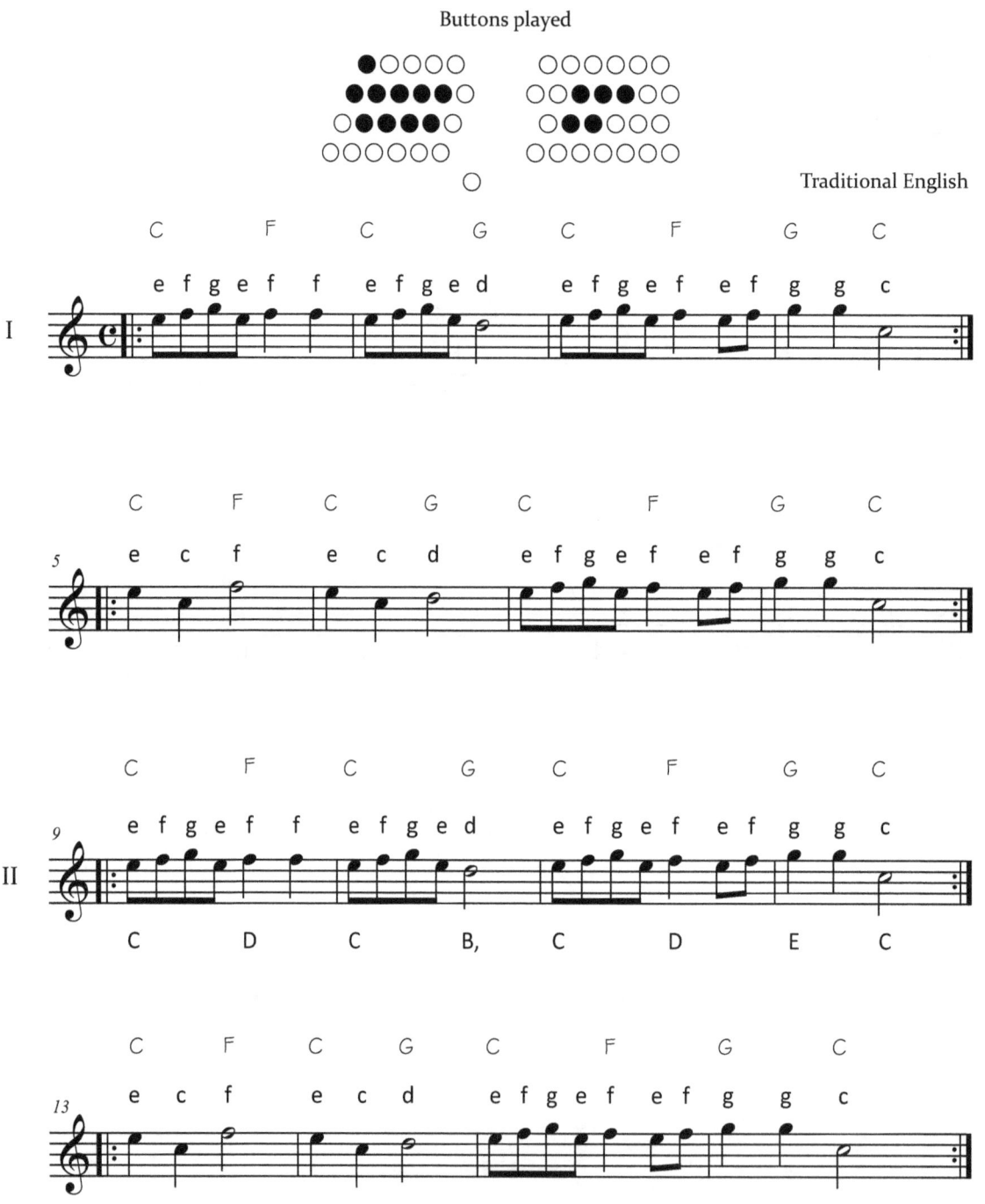

An old Scottish air dating back to the 1680's, it is the first track on Michael Hebberts' Jeffries Duet recording *The Rampin' Cat*. He also plays it in octaves with both left and right hands, which is a little tricky since the left hand "A," is not in the same pattern as the "A" on the right side.

Logan Water

Traditional Scottish (c.1816)

Here are some simple left-hand harmonies with a single note melody on the right. Believe it or not, this famous melody was composed in 1837 by Jonathan Spillman, a lawyer from Kentucky.

Flow Gently Sweet Afton

This tune was first published in 1829 as a shape note hymn called "New Britain", but it is more commonly known by its pairing in 1835 with John Newton's poem written in 1779. This will introduce you to some more bass notes plus simple chords on the left side.

Amazing Grace

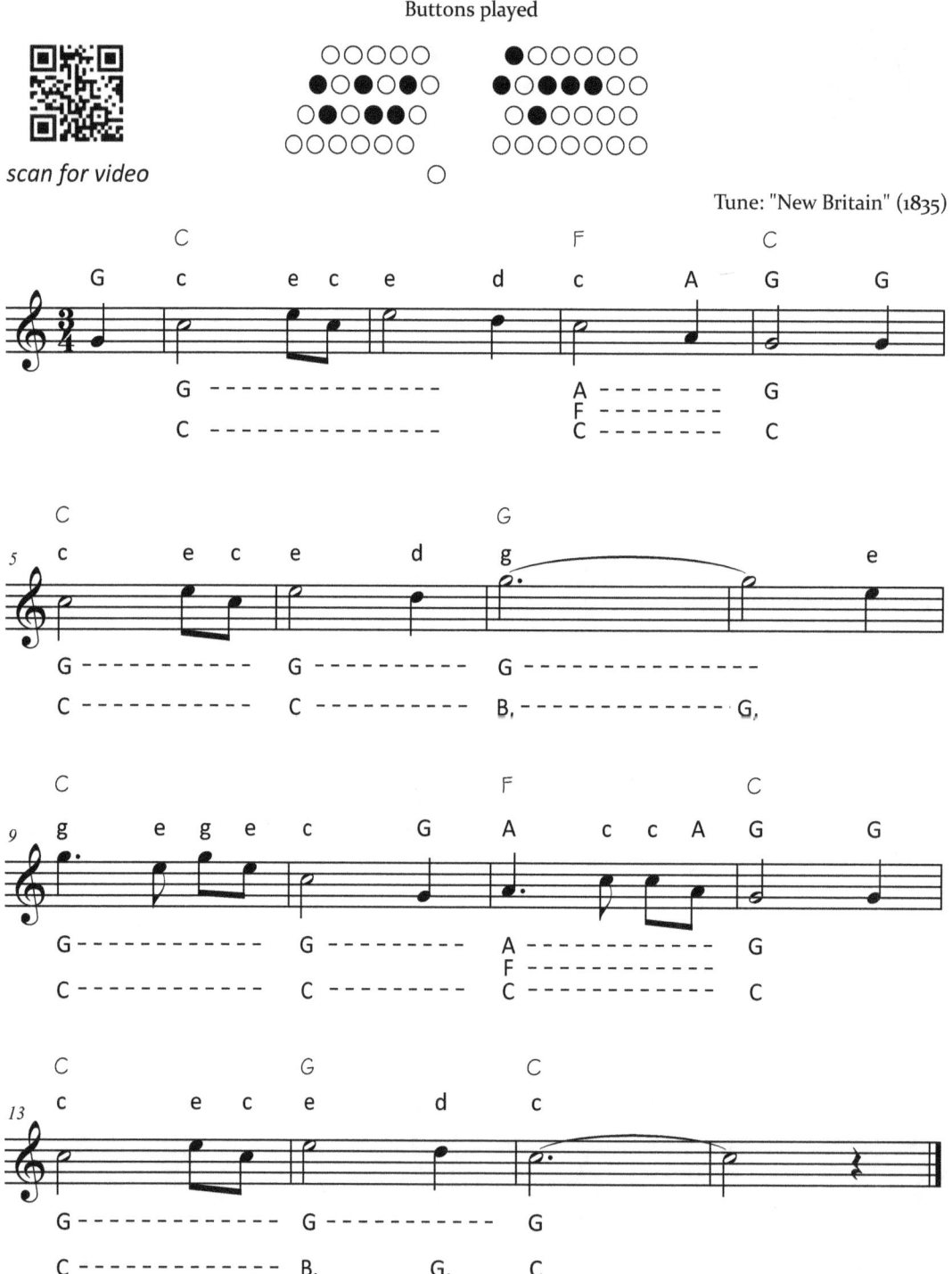

Now let's add some simple chords to "Oh Susanna" on the left-hand side – C, F and G. You will use these three chords often when playing tunes in the home key.

Oh Susanna (chords)

Stephen Foster (1848)

A traditional English Morris stick dance tune from the village of Bledington in Gloucestershire, played here with block chords – make them short and snappy like sticks clashing.

Young Collins

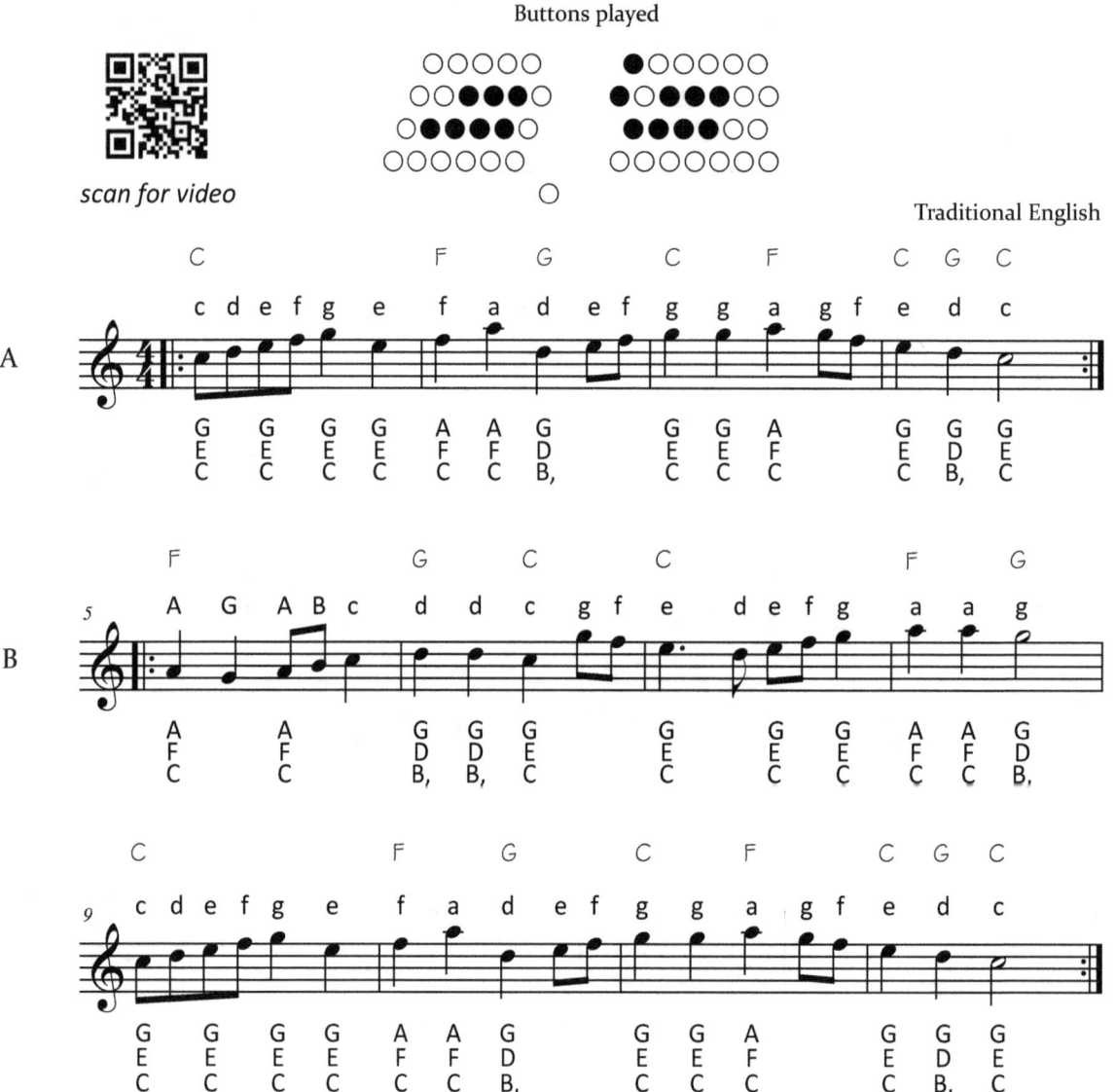

Now let's open up those chords and add dynamics with some oom-pah:

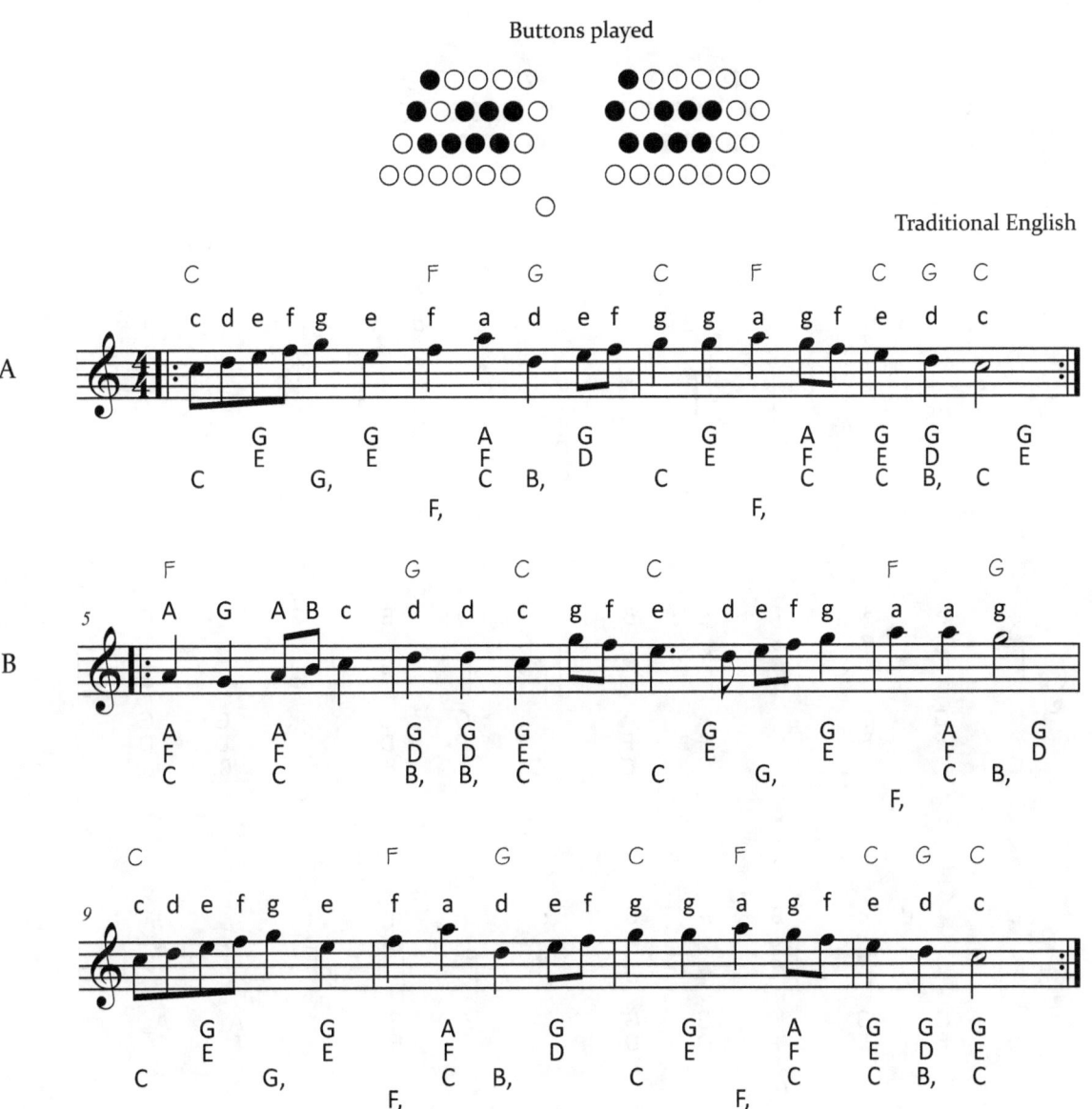

The Jeffries Duet is ideally suited for playing waltzes, here's a lovely traditional one from England.

The Man in the Moon

A traditional English Christmas carol that incorporates two apocryphal tales: "King Herod and the Cock" and "The Miraculous Harvest." Introducing the high "c'" on the right side and the low "C," on the left side.

King Pharim

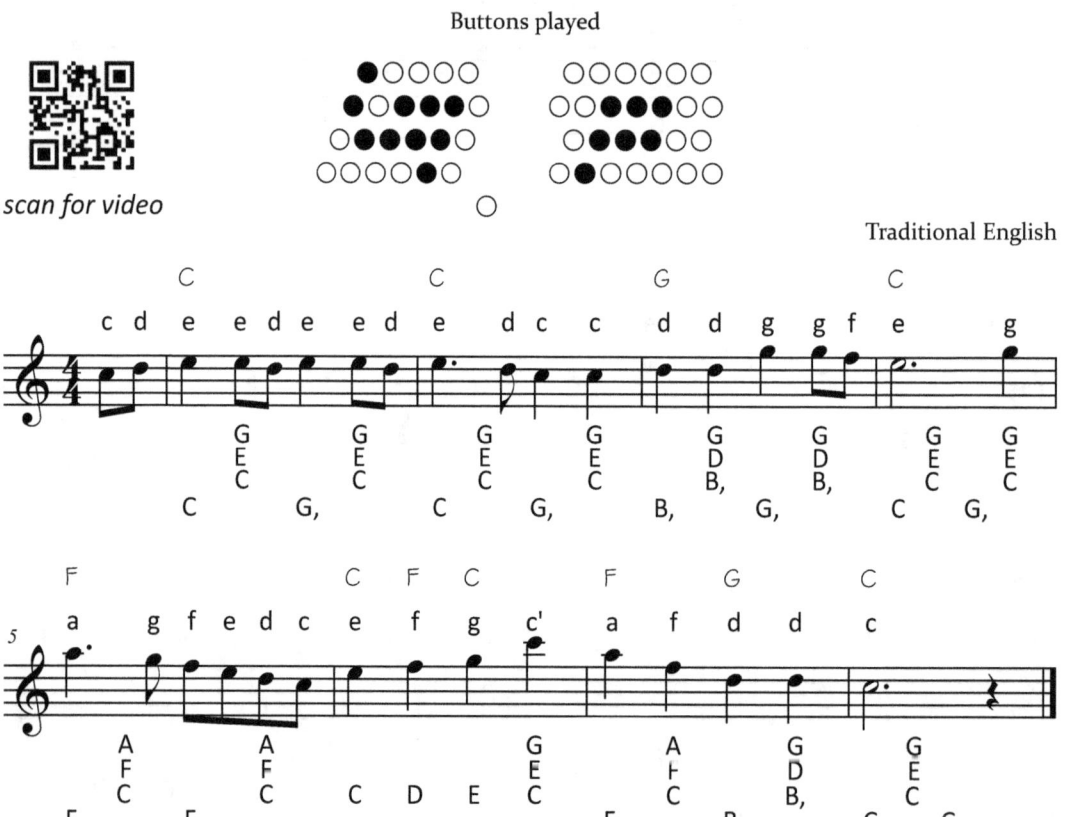

Traditional English

Translated as "old home" or "hometown", this well-known Japanese children's song was composed in 1914 by Teiichi Okano.

Furusato

Music by Teiichi Okano (1914)

Found in the log of the whaling ship *Catalpa* in 1856, and learned from the singing of A.L. Lloyd on the *Leviathan* album.

The Whaleman's Lament

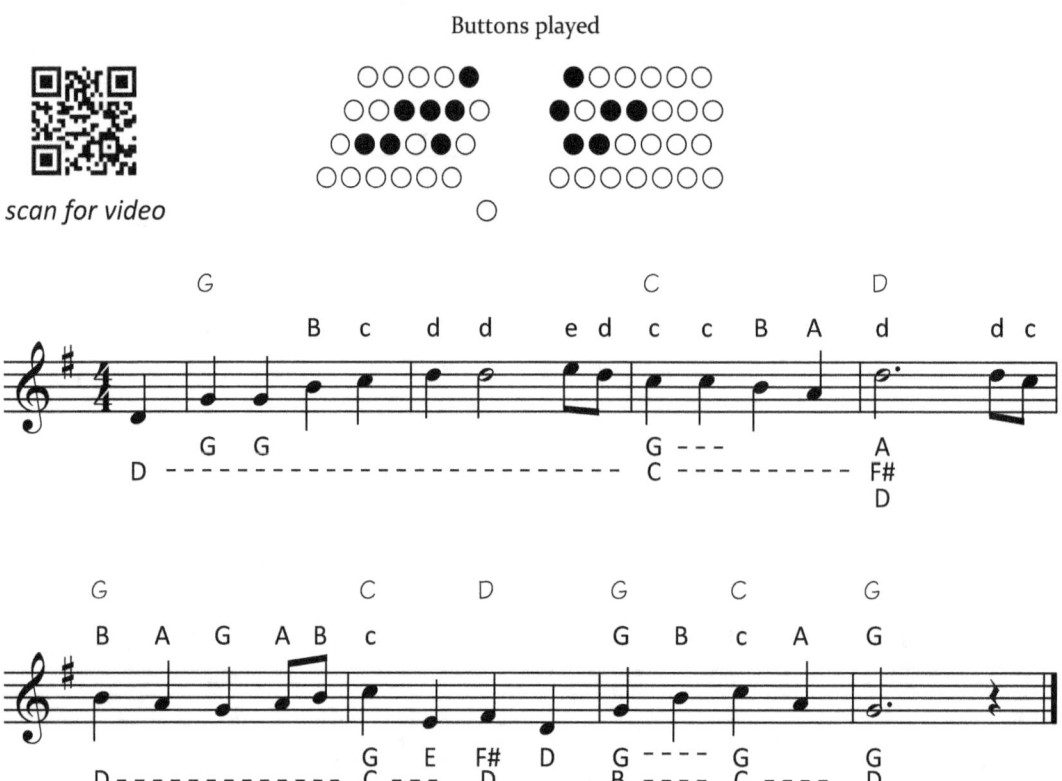

This beautiful melody was first published by Jack Thorp in 1908 as heard in a cow camp near Fort Sumner, New Mexico on the Pecos River. Learned from the singing of Roy Rogers.

The Cowman's Prayer

The Jeffries Duet Concertina Tutor

A hauntingly beautiful tune by Steve Hartz from Nacogdoches, Texas.

Rose of the Redlands

The Jeffries Duet Concertina Tutor

An old traditional Scottish melody to which Robert Burns added the words from his poem.

Auld Lang Syne

A traditional English Morris dance tune from the Cotswolds. The fancy bass notes in the B part will definitely have your little finger hopping about.

The Blue-Eyed Stranger

scan for video

Traditional English

The Jeffries Duet Concertina Tutor

Published in 1863 with words by Charles C. Sawyer and music by Henry Tucker, this song was so popular and so moving it was banned in many of the Civil War military camps.

Weeping, Sad and Lonely
(When This Cruel War is Over)

Music by Henry Tucker (1863)

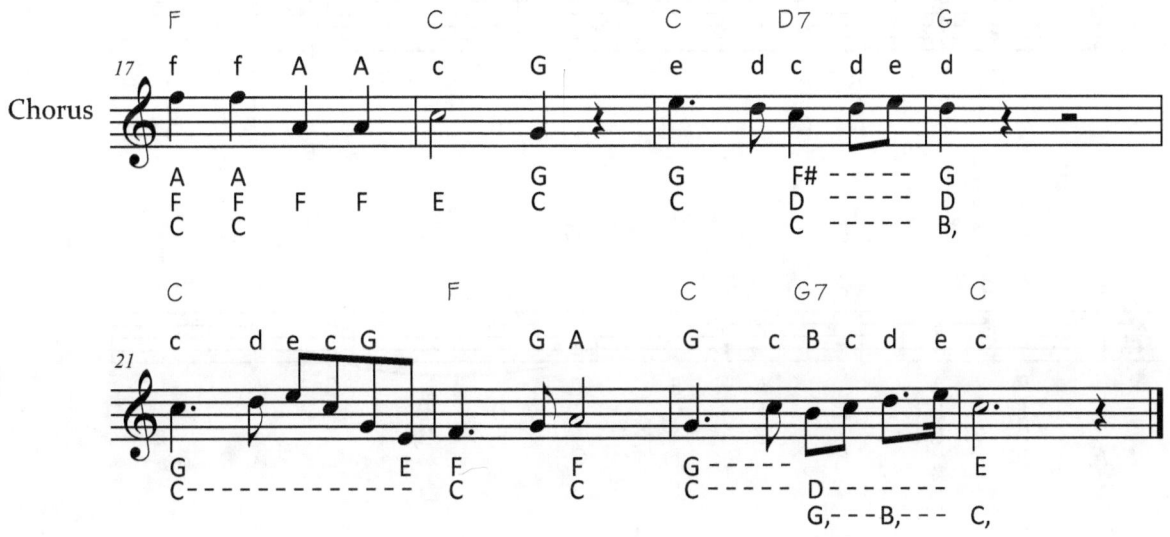

One of the most popular old Irish waltzes, only slightly different from the version on *The Rampin' Cat*.

The Star of the County Down

B
18
C C G G
g e e d c d d d c d
G G G G G G G G
E E E E D D D D
C G, B, B, G, B, B,
22
Am F G7
e d c A G c B
A A A E G G
E E F C D D
C C C B, B,
A, F, G, G, A, B,
26
Am F C G
A A A G A B c c d c d
A A A A G G G G
E E F F E E D D
C C C C C B, B, B,
A, F,
30
Am F G Am 1. Am Dm 2.
e d c A G A e f G
A A A G A A E A A A
E E F D E E D F E E
C C C B, C C C D C C
A, F, A, A, A,

A new tune in the style of an old English Morris dance.

Miss Smith's Morris

Gary Coover

Copyright © Gary Coover
Used with permission. All rights reserved.

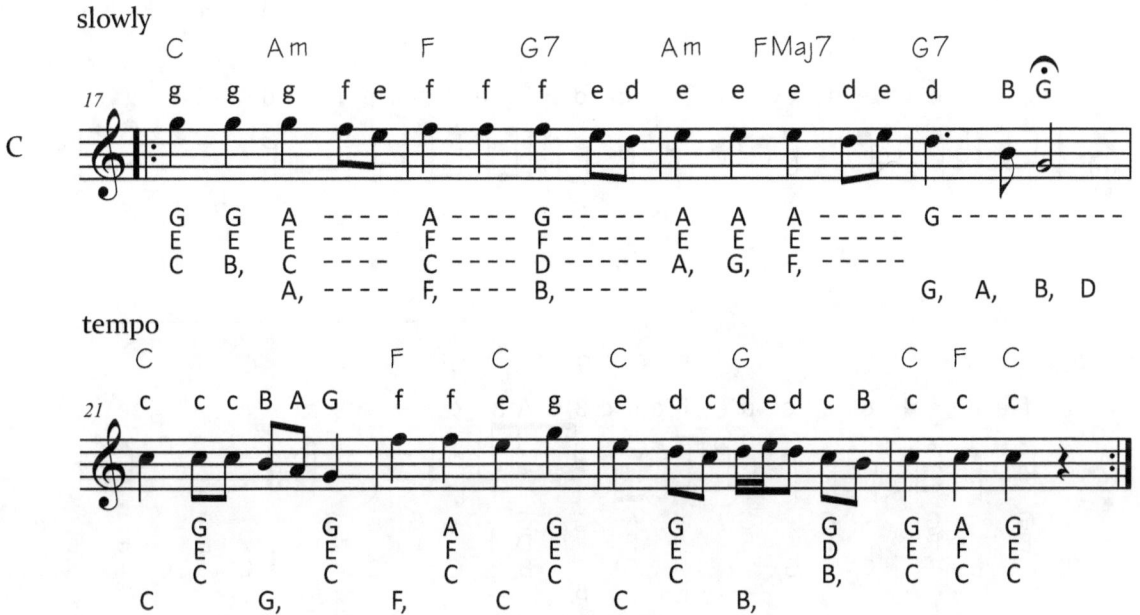

Copyright © Gary Coover
Used with permission. All rights reserved.

A traditional English country dance tune that is great fun to play on the Jeffries Duet. Once you know these 21 buttons (2 ½ octaves of the C scale) you can play an amazing number of tunes.

Galopede

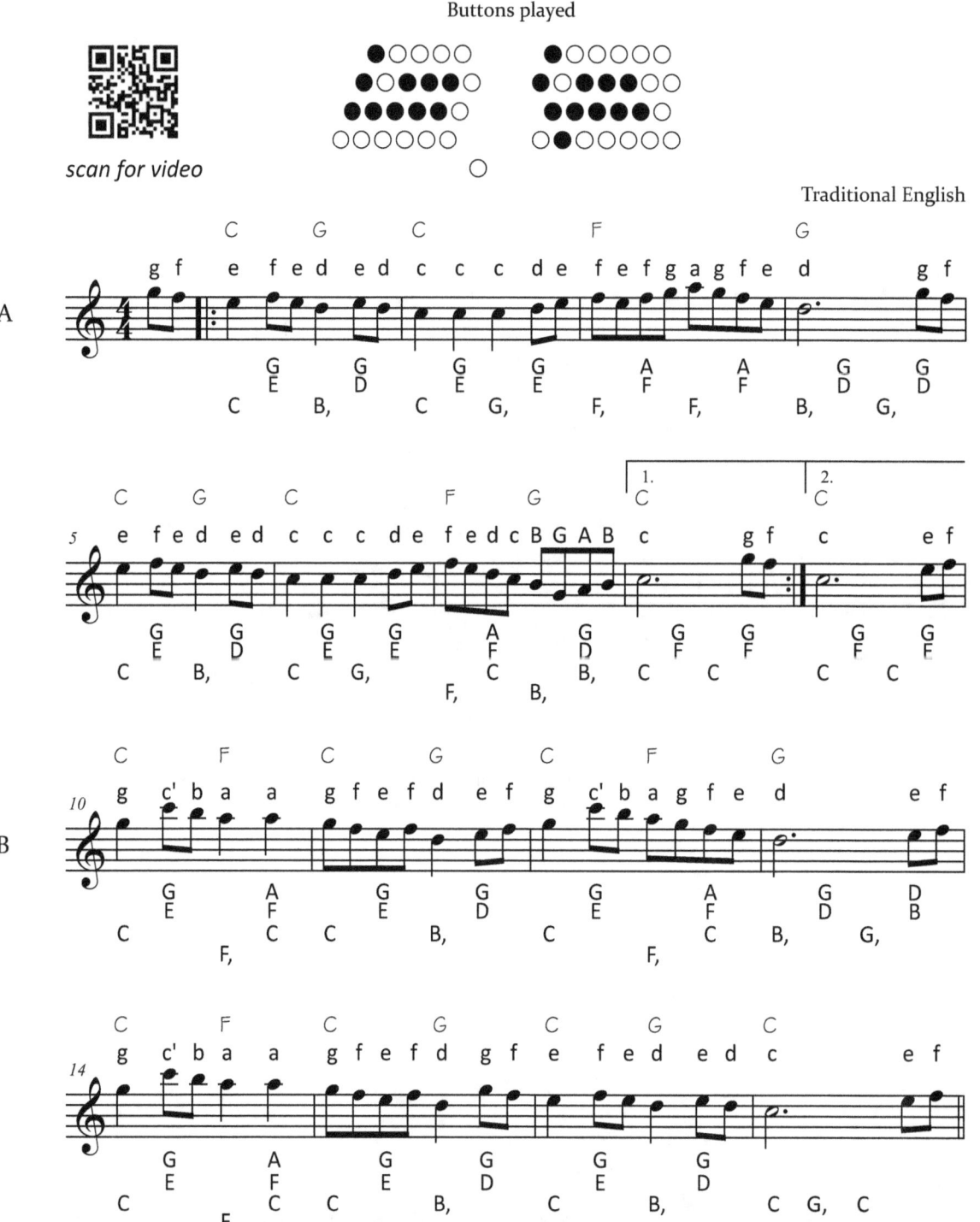

In 1906, Gustav Holst paired Christina Rossetti's 1872 poem with his tune called "Cranham".

In the Bleak Midwinter

First published in 1841 as "The Bonnie Banks o' Loch Lomond" (author unknown) and using drones on the left side to mimic the sound of the Scottish bagpipes.

Loch Lomond

This is a popular Northumbrian rant from northeast England and a favorite of Northumbrian pipers. Transcribed from the Jeffries Duet playing of Erik House.

Salmontails Up the Water

Buttons played

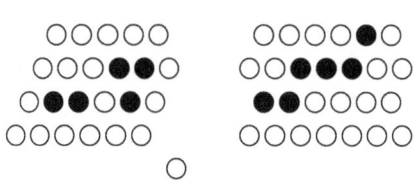

Traditional Northumbrian

This is the English country dance version of a popular jig also known as "Merrily Kissed the Quaker" or "Merrily Kissed the Quaker's Wife". From the playing of Michael Hebbert on *The Rampin' Cat*.

The Quaker's Wife

An Irish jig from the Jeffries Duet playing of Erik House.

Kate's Rambles

Buttons played

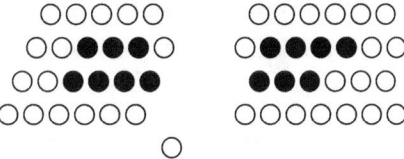

Traditonal Irish

A

B
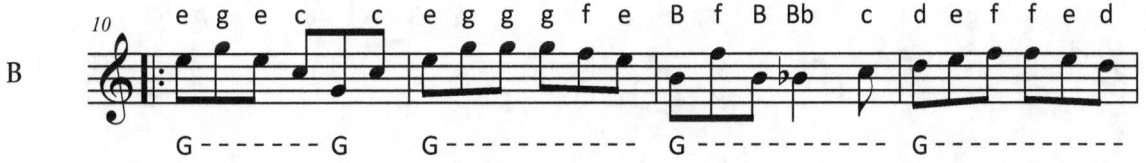

Composed by Dave Leggett, a concertina player from Cornwall, England.

The Gurnard Waltz

Copyright © Dave Leggett
Used with permission. All rights reserved.

A Quebecois tune that modulates from Am to C to F, composed in the early 1920's by the legendary accordion player Alfred Montmarquette. From the Jeffries Duet playing of Erik House.

Alfred Montmarquette's 6/8

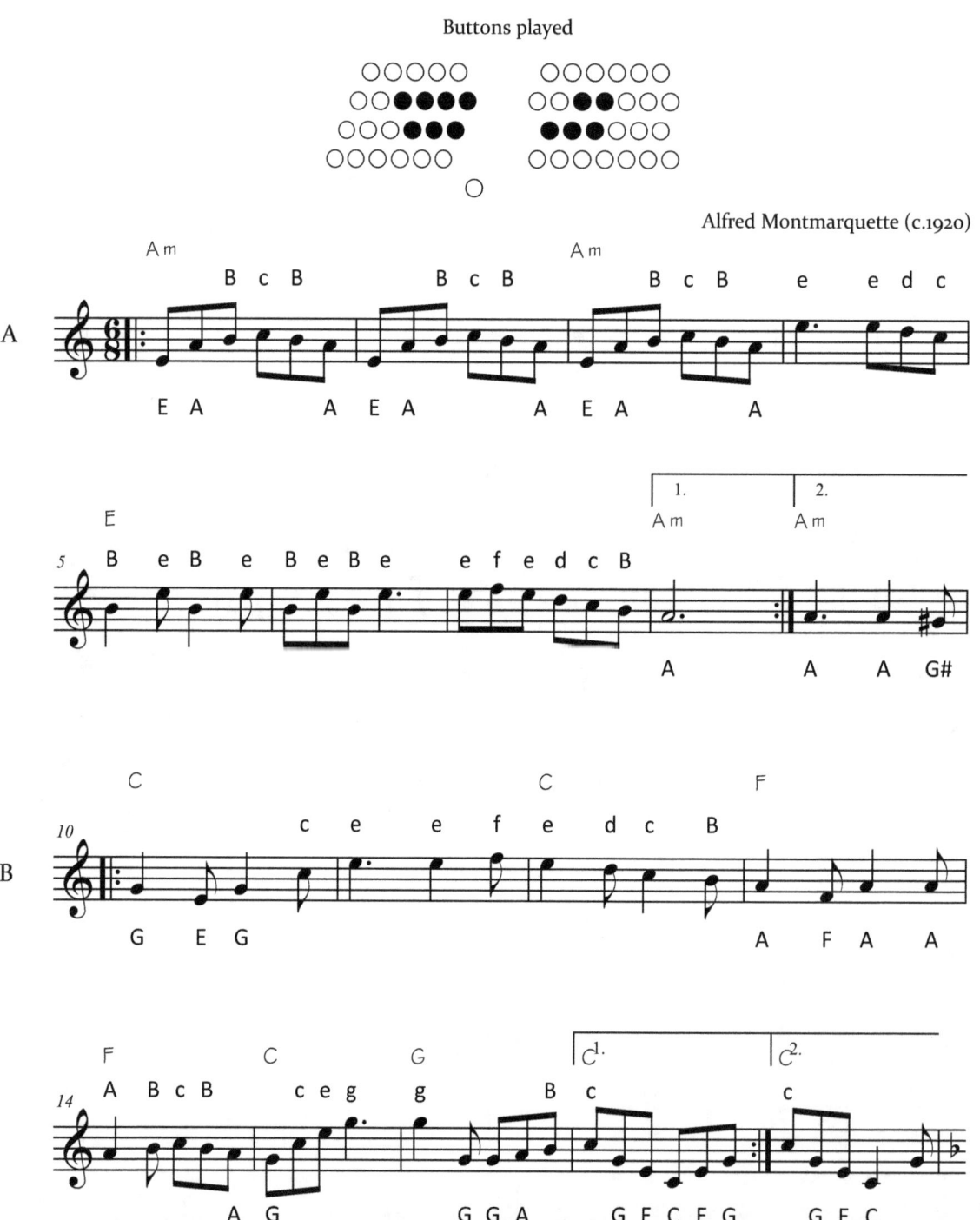

Collected by Cecil Sharp in 1908 from Anglo concertina player William Kimber in Headington Quarry, Oxfordshire.

Country Gardens

Traditional English

A classic American folk song from the early 1800's, including some nice left-hand bass note walkdowns and walkups.

Shenandoah

Traditional American

From Mike Oldfield's 1976 hit recording of this traditional Christmas carol. And yes, if you pick out the electric guitar solo on the recording you'll find it fits very nicely on the Jeffries Duet.

In Dulci Jubilo

English, c.1400

Here's a traditional Australian tune that is good for learning the notes higher up on the right-hand side outside the central sawtooth.

The Mudgee Waltz

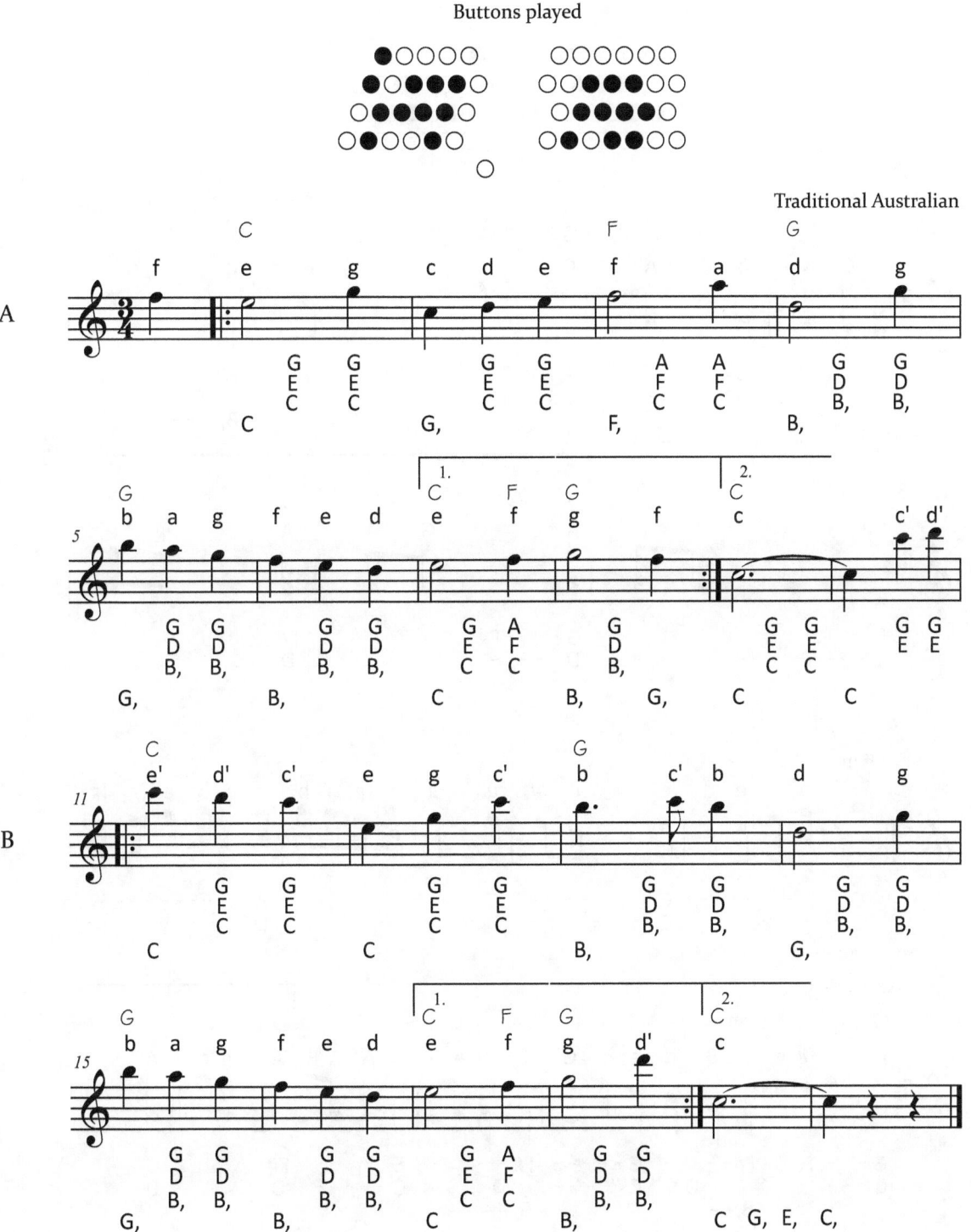

An Irish harp tune composed by Turlough O'Carolan. To be played very slowly and expressively.

Eleanor Plunkett

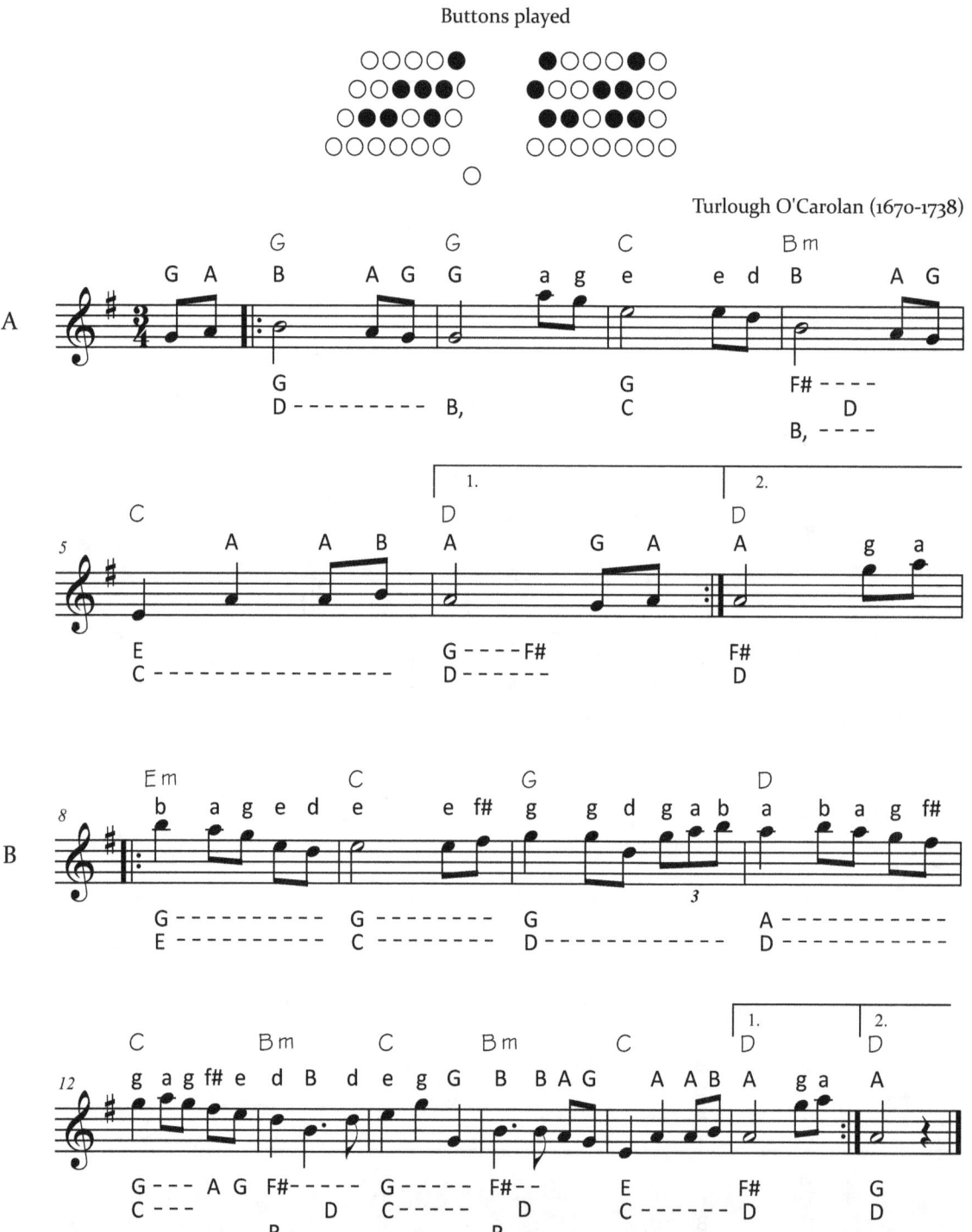

A traditional Irish hornpipe played mostly on the left hand. Be sure to play the notes in a dotted hornpipe rhythm. From the Jeffries Duet playing of Erik House.

Rights of Man

Buttons played

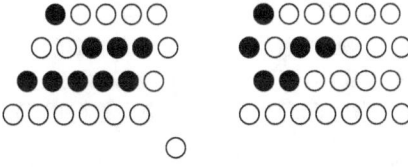

Traditional Irish

A traditional English Morris Dance tune from the village of Bucknell, Oxfordshire, and learned from the accordion playing of Denis Smith with the Westminster Morris Men.

The Queen's Delight

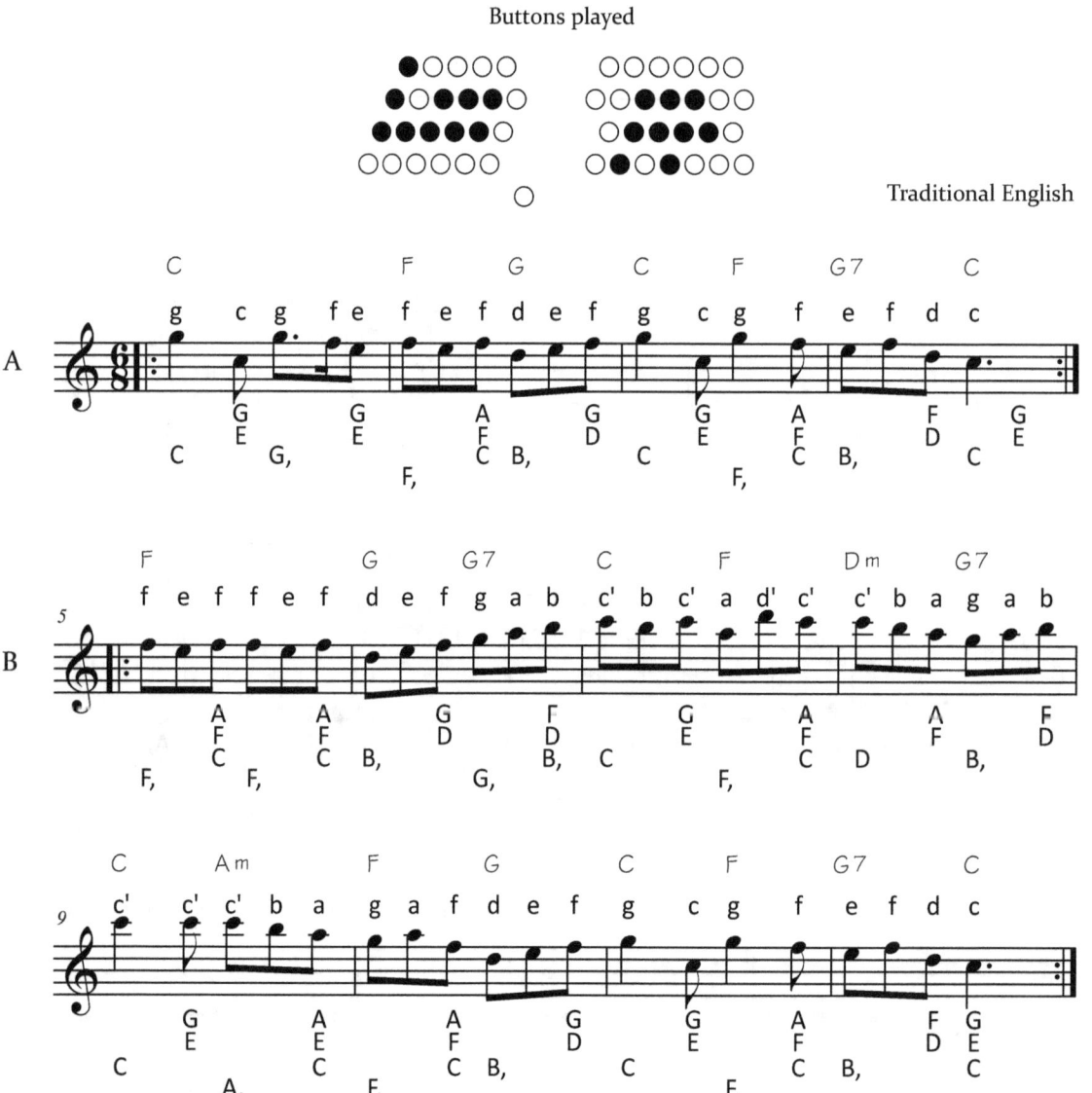

Traditional English

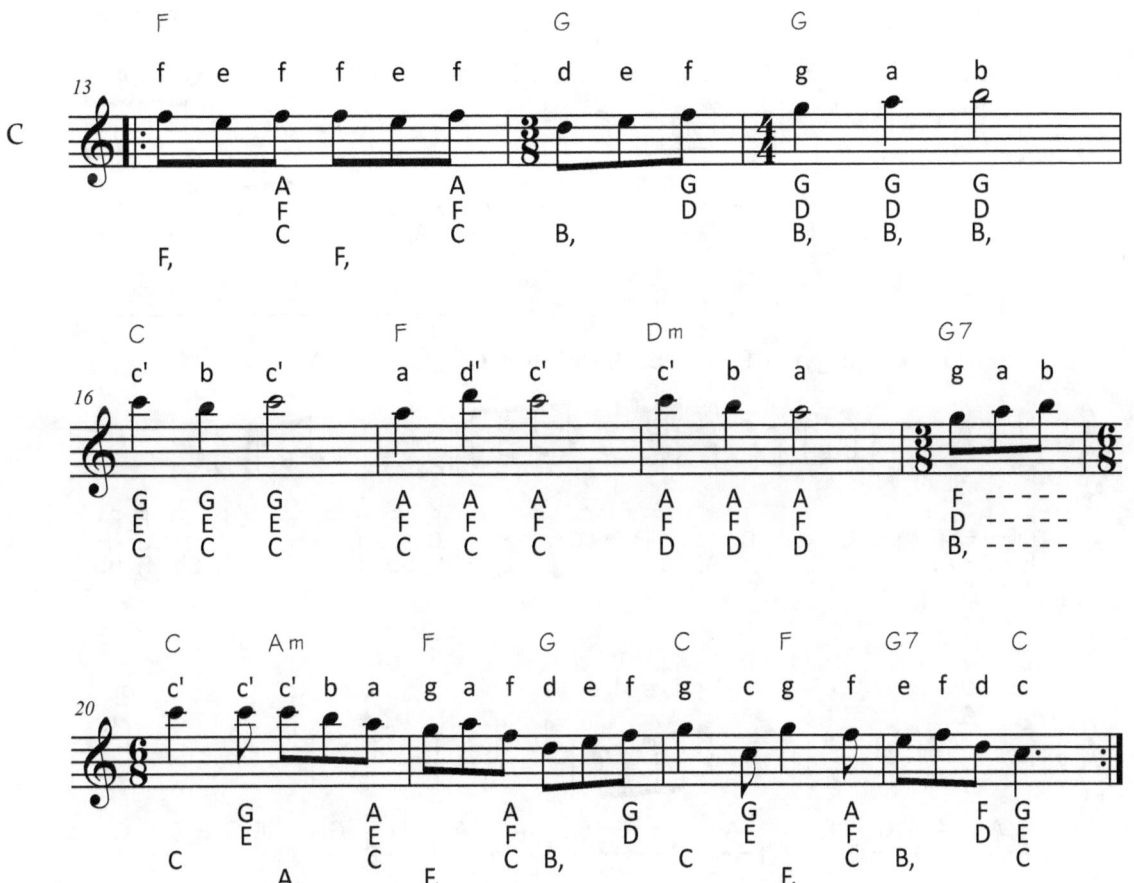

Perhaps the most beautiful of Shetland fiddler Tom Anderson's many composed tunes, inspired by the depopulation of his birthplace, Eshaness. "Slockit" is a Shetland word for a light that has gone out. From the Jeffries Duet playing of Stuart Estell.

Da Slockit Light

Tom Anderson (1969)

Copyright © Shetland Musical Heritage Trust
Used with permission. All rights reserved.

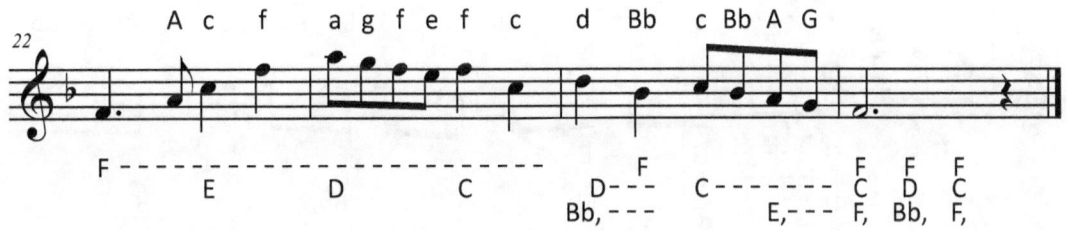

Copyright © Shetland Musical Heritage Trust
Used with permission. All rights reserved.

From *Kerr's Third Collection of Merrie Melodies* published c.1875, and transcribed from the playing of Michael Hebbert on *The Rampin' Cat*.

American Boot Dance

Traditional

Written by Tom Anderson for Peter Leith, owner of a wee boat and the piano player in the Isleburgh House Dance Band. From the playing of Michael Hebbert on *The Rampin' Cat*.

Peter's Peerie Boat

Copyright © Shetland Musical Heritage Trust
Used with permission. All rights reserved.

Composed by Anglo concertina player Jody Kruskal and transcribed from the Jeffries Duet playing of Nick Robertshaw.

Procrastination Waltz

An English Morris tune from the village of Fieldtown (Leafield) in Oxfordshire, learned from the melodeon playing of Shag Graetz.

Dearest Dickie

Traditional English

One of the great Scottish highland bagpipe tunes, composed by William Lawrie who was wounded in the Battle of the Somme in July 1916 as Pipe Major of the 8th Argyllshire Battalion. He unfortunately died of his injuries four months later.

The Battle of the Somme

Pipe Major William Laurie (1916)

One of many fine new tunes in the old-time style by Steve Hartz from the Piney Woods of East Texas. Play it briskly like a fast march.

Old Magnolia

A well-known regimental quick march from Michael Hebbert's *The Rampin' Cat*, where it was listed as "Untitled" in the medley that starts with "Auld Donald". Play the chords very quickly and very staccato, barely tapping them while concentrating on the rhythm and the melody.

Merry Month of May

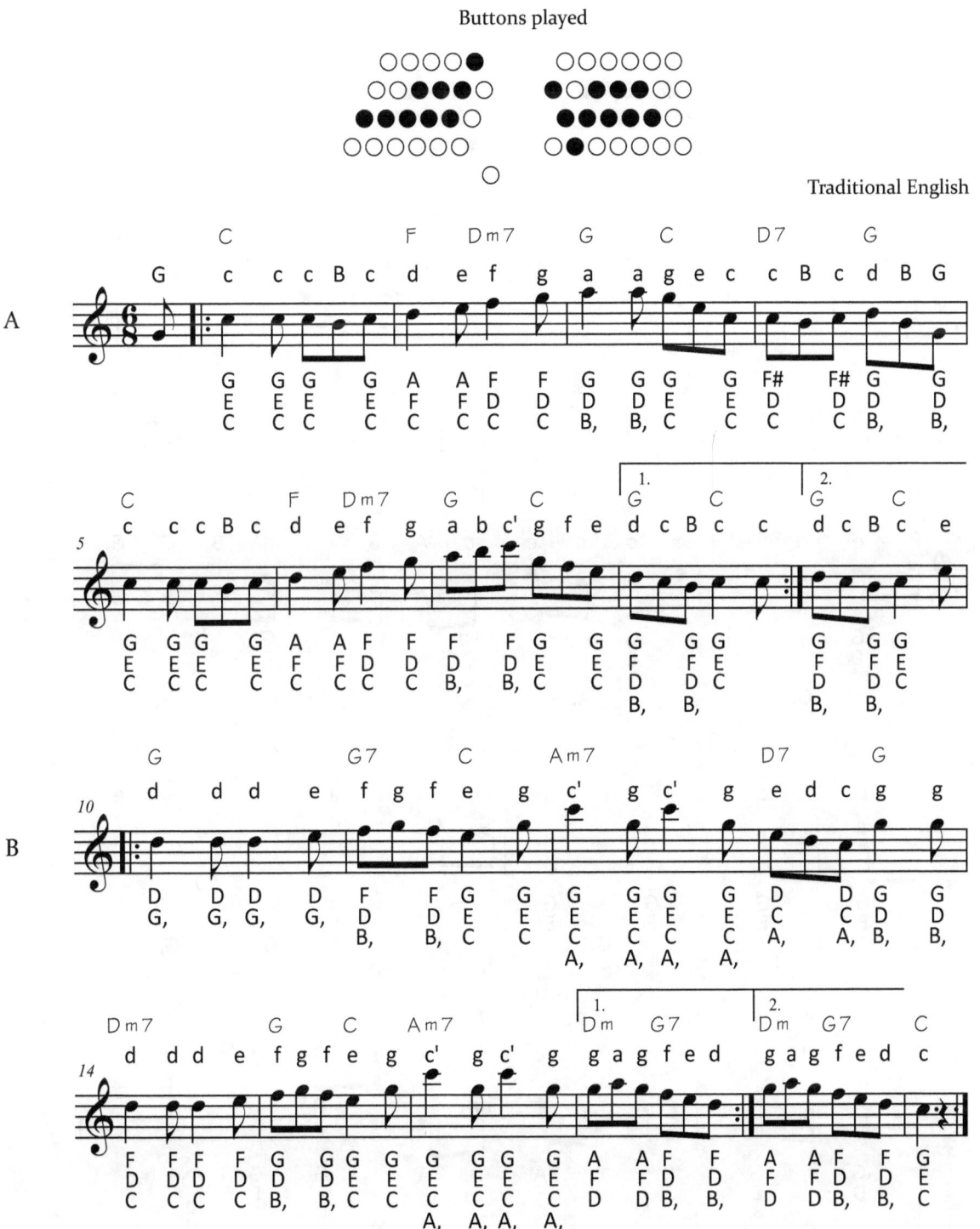

Adapted by Kerry Mills from Robert Schumann's "Happy Farmer" in 1907, and learned from my father's harmonica playing.

Red Wing

One of the most popular Swedish tunes, this is a "walking tune" for processionals that comes from the village of Gärdeby. It is pronounced something like "yairrr-deh-bee-loh-ten". From the Jeffries Duet playing of Erik House.

Gärdebylåten

Buttons played

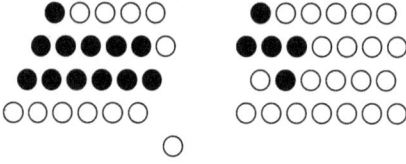

Traditional Swedish

A, Bb, C D C A, C D C A, C F A G F E D D E D B, D E D B, D A Bb A G F E
F,   Bb,

E F E D C C A Bb A G F   F   E F E F A   G E G C   A, Bb,
C   C

C D C A, C D C A, C F A G F E D D E D B, D E D B, D A Bb A G F E
                                 Bb,   Bb,   Bb,

E F E D C C A Bb A G F F E E G F E F C F, A Bb
C

Just the top two lines from page 67 of *The Methodist Hymnal* (1939).

A Mighty Fortress is our God

Martin Luther (1483-1546)

One of the most famous of all traditional Irish tunes, to which the words to "Danny Boy", written by Frederic Weatherly, were added in 1913.

Londonderry Air

Traditional Irish

The Jeffries Duet Concertina Tutor

Written by the late Jeffries Duet player Nick Robertshaw. See the "Videos and Recordings" section for a link to a video of Nick performing the song live.

Hell Ship

SHE'S A HELL SHIP WITH A BULLY MATE
A BASTARD SON OF MALICE AND HATE
AND THE CAPTAIN'S THE CRUELEST EVER WAS BORN
AND TOGETHER WE'RE SAILING ROUND CAPE HORN

O sailors take heed, you better beware
Of a treacherous whore named Molly Blaire
In the taproom at the Rose and Crown
On the dockside down in Gravesend town

While she dizzies you with her smiles and charms
And tumbles you merrily in her arms
She'll be slipping drops into your ale
Then you'll find you've shipped on the Abigail

When you wake you find you're far from shore
With no boots or jacket and a head so sore
And the tyrants ruling over the crew
With the fist and the cat and the black-jack too

If the first mate he don't like your face
You might find yourself in a far worse place
At the bottom of the sea with your head stoved in
By a capstan bar or belaying pin

Off Magellan Straits under mountain seas
We're starved and sick and we damn near freeze
Stood for fourteen days as any can tell
In the gale that blows from the arse of hell

If ever I see dry land once more
I'll jump from the pinrail and swim ashore
And be damned sure that I nevermore sail
On a hell ship like the Abigail

An unusual setting of this traditional English tune learned from the playing of the Etchingham Steam Band.

Portsmouth (Setting 1)

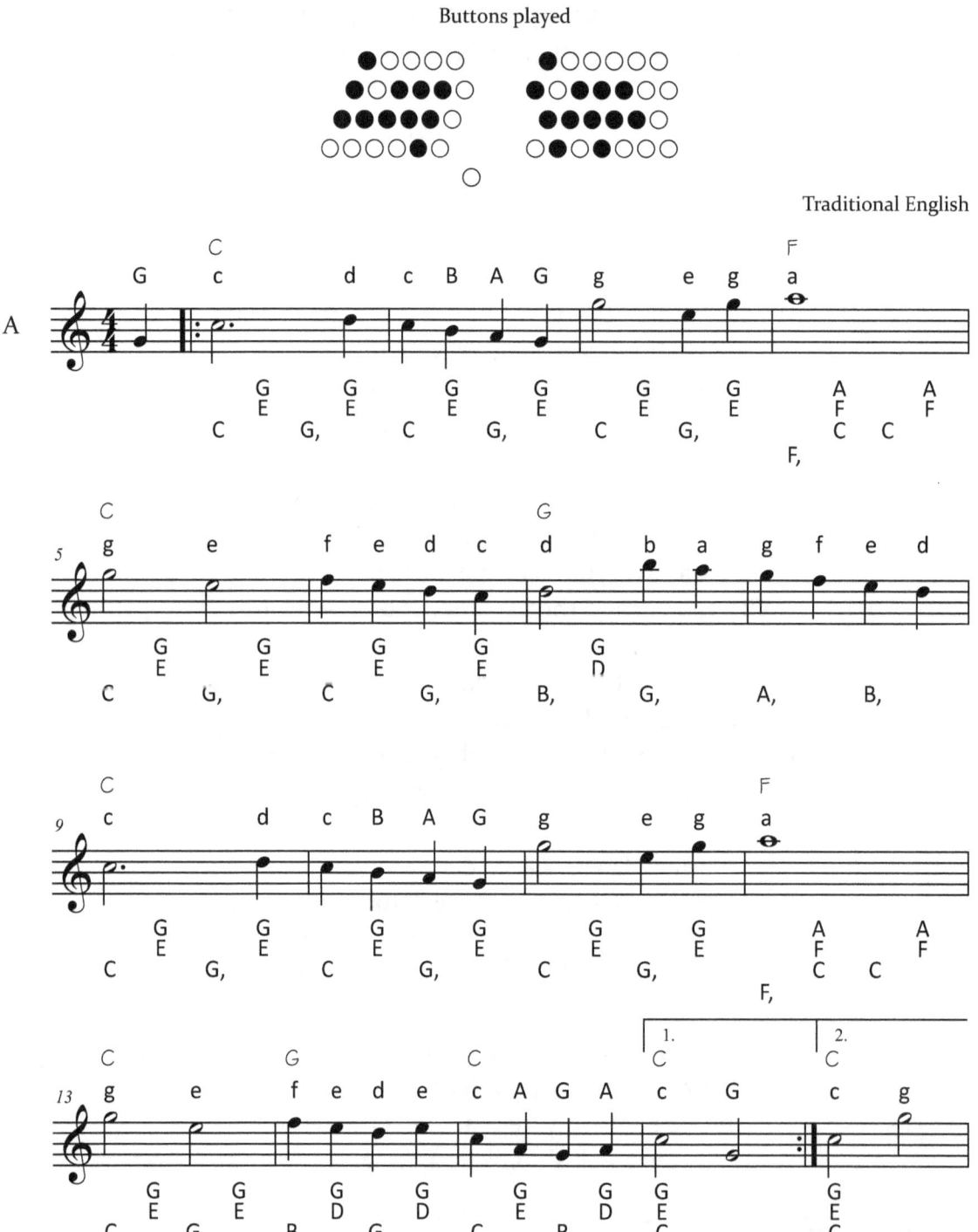

Traditional English

Here is the more common version, from the 11th edition of John Playford's *The Dancing Master* (1701) and made into a pop hit by Mike Oldfield in 1976.

Portsmouth (Setting 2)

First published in the 9th edition of Playford's *Dancing Master* (1695) by Henry Playford. From the playing of Michael Hebbert on *The Rampin' Cat*.

The Indian Queen

A traditional Scottish air based on the playing of Michael Hebbert on *The Rampin' Cat*.

Auld Donald

An English country dance learned from the melodeon playing of Clive Williams.

Three Around Three

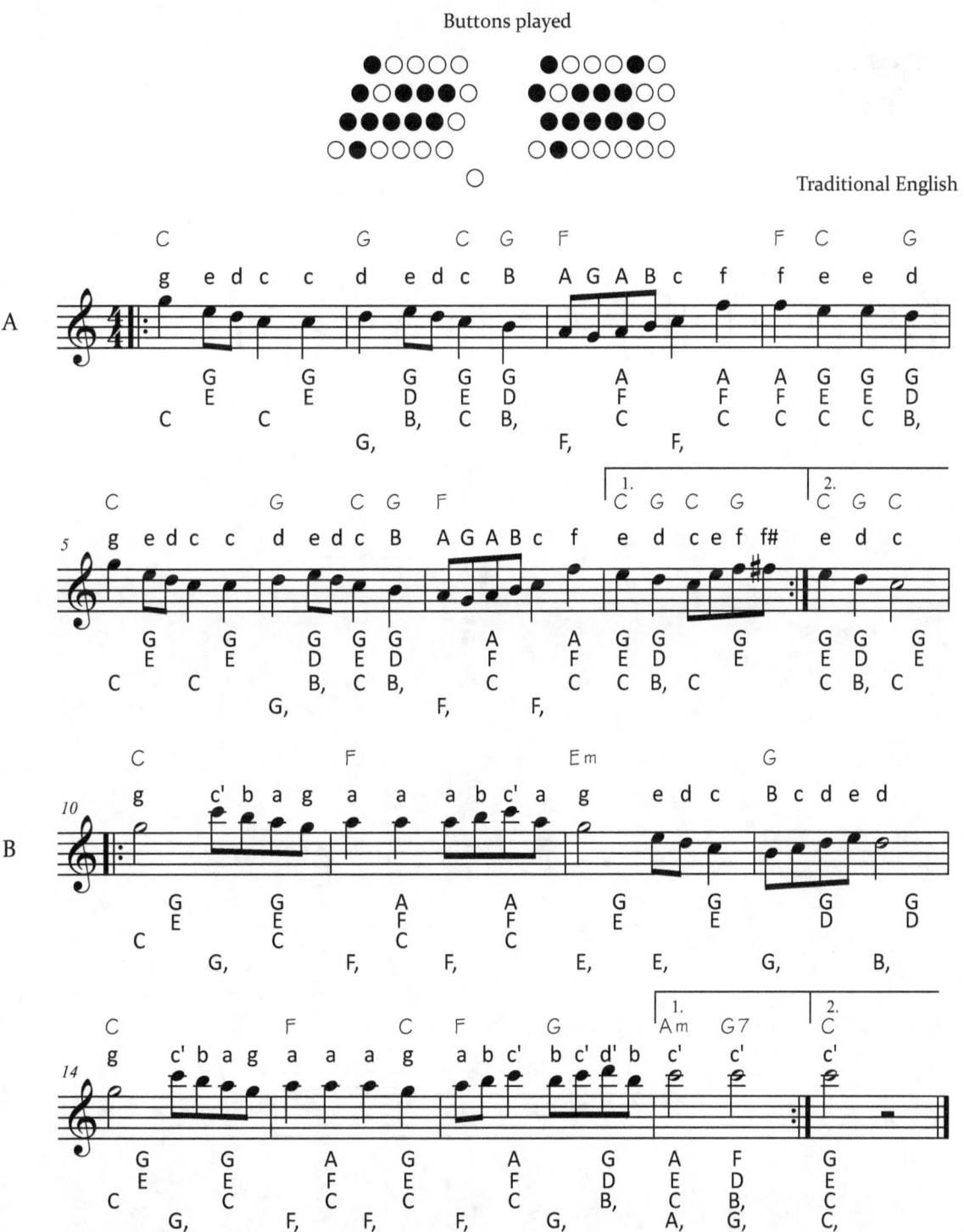

A classic hymn with words written in 1855 and the tune composed by Charles Crozat Converse in 1868. Played here in a Southern Gospel style.

What a Friend We Have in Jesus

Humorously titled "Gathering Codpieces" on *The Rampin' Cat*, this English country dance was first printed by John Playford in 1651. The C part is particularly fun to play on the Jeffries Duet.

Gathering Peascods

Playford (1651)

A classic patriotic march written by Frank W. Meacham in 1885 and later made famous by Glenn Miller and his orchestra. Learned from an old LP of calliope music from Sikeston, Missouri.

The American Patrol

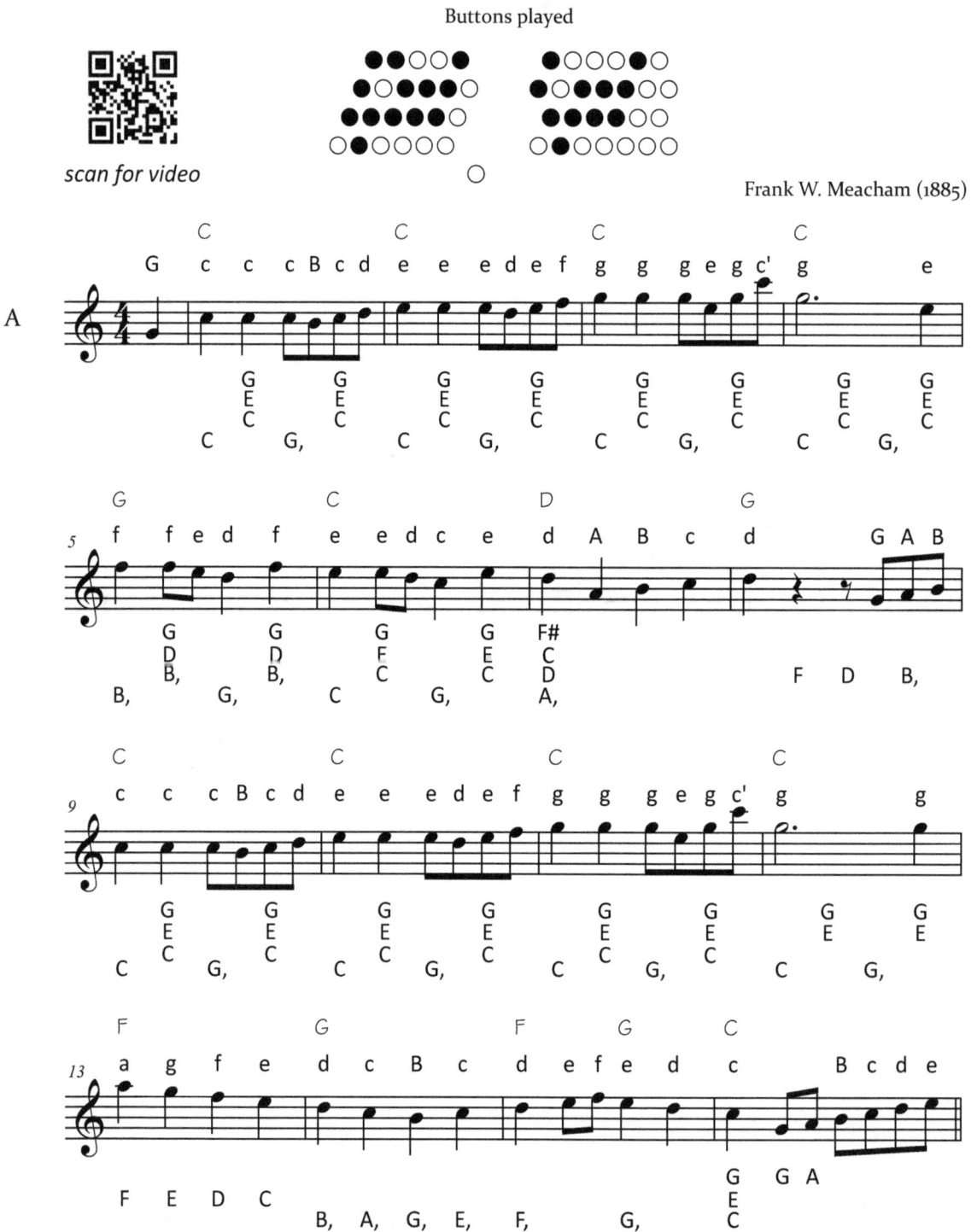

Frank W. Meacham (1885)

A traditional American tune in the key of D learned from music sessions with hammered dulcimer players Dana Hamilton and David Lindsey from central Texas.

Angeline the Baker (D)

Now that you've struggled with playing it in D, see how much more easy and fun it is to play in the home key of C.

Angeline the Baker (C)

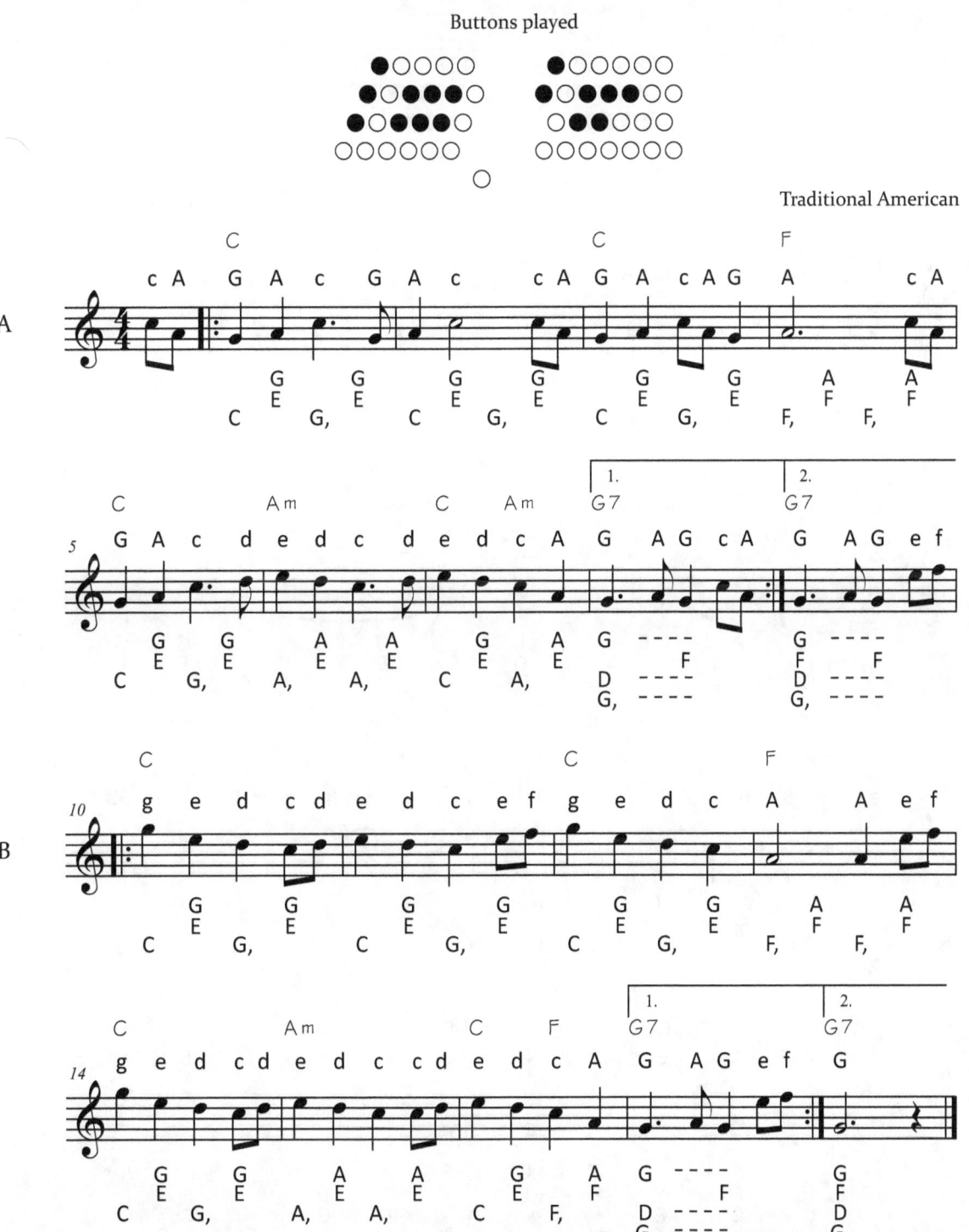

A traditional tune from the Orkney Islands from the playing of Michael Hebbert on *The Rampin' Cat*, in the key of F.

Orkney Rope Waltz

A musical piece in the 1725 Notebook for Anna Magdalena Bach that is from a harpsichord suite by Dresden organist Christian Petzold. Reaching the f-sharp notes are the difficult part about playing in the key of G. On this one you get to use your left thumb and also hit the lowest note.

Minuet in G

Buttons played

J.S. Bach

```
     d  G A B c d  G  G   e  c d e f# g  G  G
G, ------ A,   B, --------- C ----------- B, ---------
```

```
   c  d c B A B  c B A G  F#  G A B G  B  A
A, ----------- G, ----------- D   R,  G,   D   D, C B, A,
```

```
     d  G A B c d  G  G   e  c d e f# g  G  G
B, ------ A,  G,  B, G,  C ----------- B,  C B, A, G,
```

```
   c  d c B A B  c B A G  A  B A G F# G
A, ------ F#,   G, ------ B,   C  D  A,   G,  G,,
```

One of my father's favorite songs, with words written by Carl Boberg in 1885, but I'll bet he'd be really surprised to learn Boberg's poem was set to a traditional Swedish melody.

How Great Thou Art

Traditional Swedish

The Jeffries Duet Concertina Tutor

Classic Tin Pan Alley Irish sentimentality, including the verse which almost nobody knows.

My Wild Irish Rose

Chauncey Olcott (1899)

Chorus

The Jeffries Duet Concertina Tutor

Another Irish classic from Tin Pan Alley, from 112, complete with original verse.

When Irish Eyes Are Smiling

The Jeffries Duet Concertina Tutor

Translated as "The Moon Over the Deserted Castle" and composed by Rentaro Taki in 1901. From the Jeffries Duet playing of Hidetoshi Yamashita.

Kojo no Tsuki
(The Moon Over the Deserted Castle)

Rentaro Taki (1901)

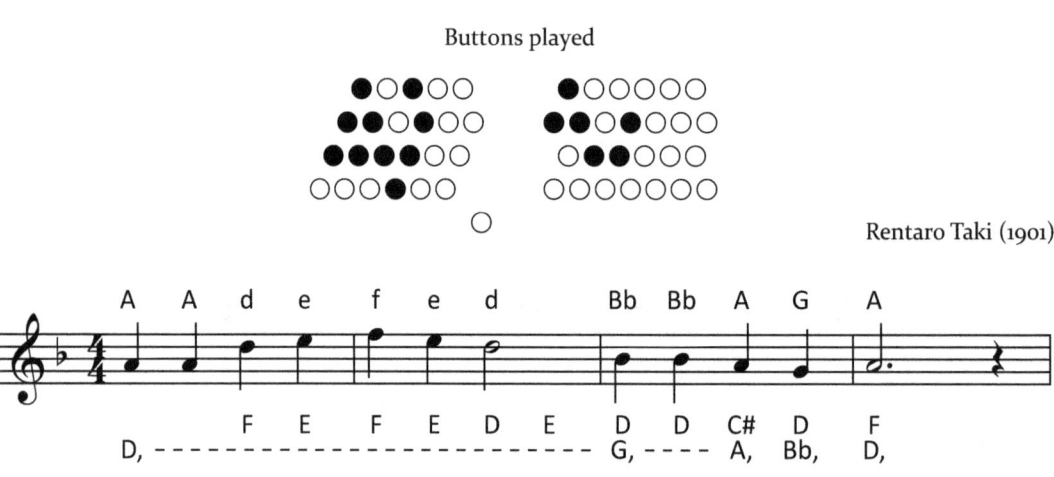

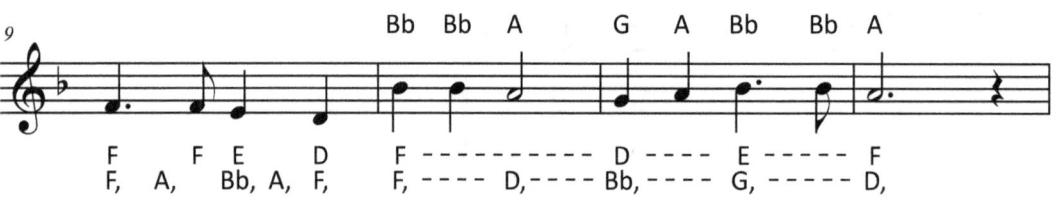

The Jeffries Duet Concertina Tutor

An English country dance in the key of G from the 11th edition of Playford's *Dancing Master*, 1701. From the playing of Michael Hebbert. Play it very sprightly and very staccato.

Nottingham Castle

Written by the late "Big Nick" Robertshaw, a larger-than-life Jeffries Duet player who lived in Washington, DC. A sentiment which we can all raise our glasses to!

Beer That Tastes Like Beer

(Nick Robertshaw)

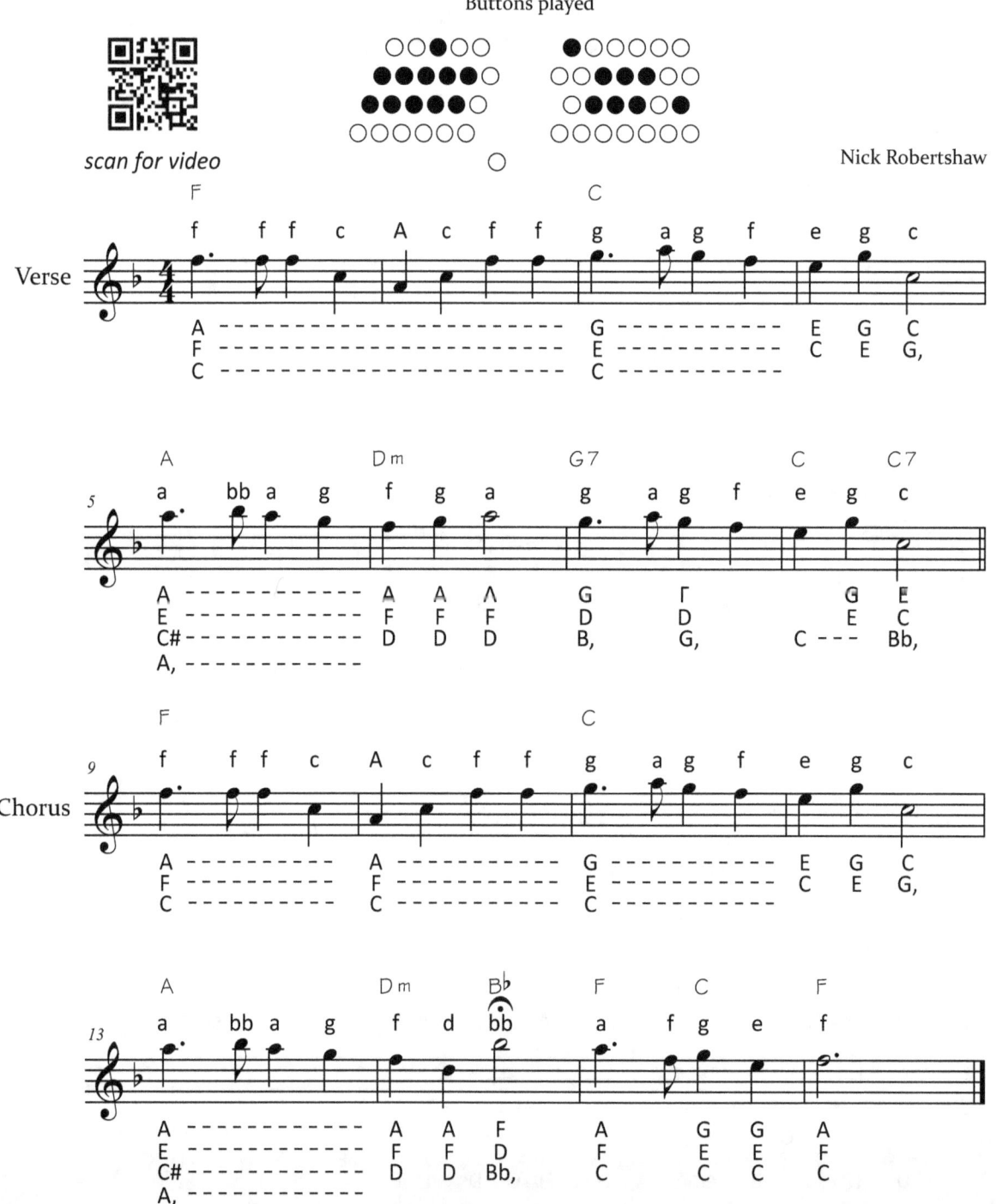

Copyright © 1999 Nick Robertshaw
Used with permission. All rights reserved.

HERE'S TO BEER THAT TASTES LIKE BEER
AN AMBER GLASS OF WHOLESOME CHEER
A NOBLE BREW THAT HAS NO PEER
BEER THAT TASTES LIKE BEER

For centuries the brewers craft
Produced the most exquisite draft
When he brews with what he oughter
Barley malt, hops, yeast and water

Let cheese be cheese and bread be bread
Don't serve us soap or sponge instead
While sausages may cause some fear
For goodness sake let beer be beer

Among the most requested favors
Please avoid exotic flavors
Fruits and nuts and spices queer
Have no place in honest beer

Oh stay the bung don't drive the spile
On concoctions rank with adjuncts vile
Cornflakes, rice and rats from sewers
Fine for cooks but not for brewers

So stick with what is good and true
A beery tasting smelling brew
Then you'll earn our highest rating
Refreshing yet intoxicating

A favorite of carousel organs, calliopes, and mechanical music boxes, the Anheuser-Busch brewing company commissioned Harry Von Tilzer to compose this song in 1903, later adapted by the British Music Hall into "Down at the Old Bull and Bush". From the original sheet music.

Under the Anheuser Busch

Music by Harry Von Tilzer (1903)

Yes, you can play bluesy tunes on the Jeffries Duet. This is the same key and arrangement from *Anglo Concertina in the Harmonic Style.*

St. James Infirmary

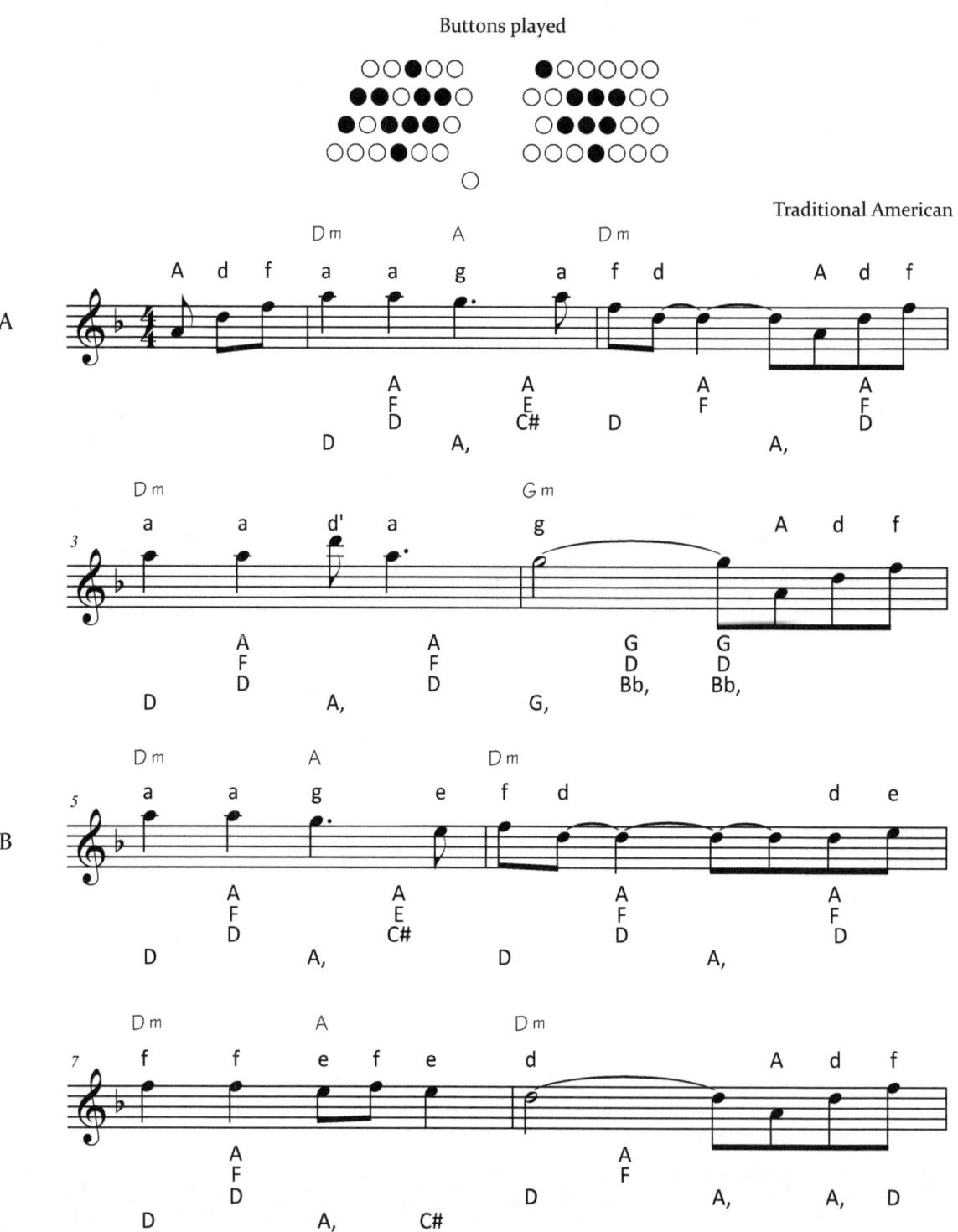

With music by Leo Friedman and lyrics by Beth Slater Whitson, this song was first published in 1910 and has been hugely popular ever since. From the original sheet music.

Let Me Call You Sweetheart

Buttons played

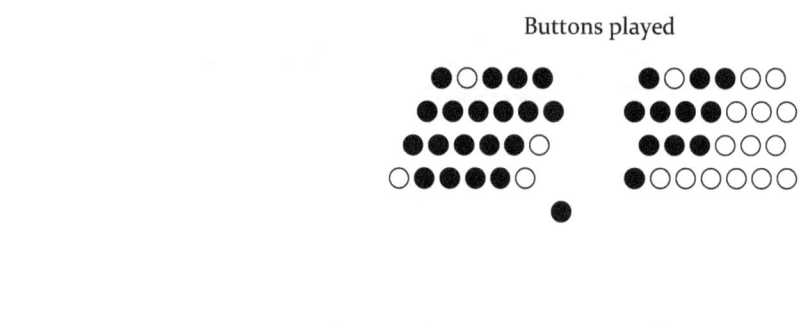

Music by Leo Friedman (1910)

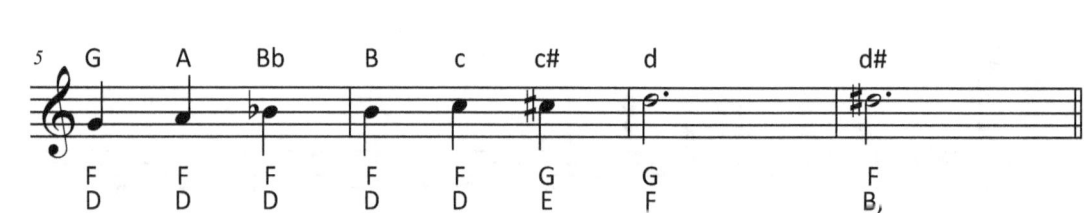

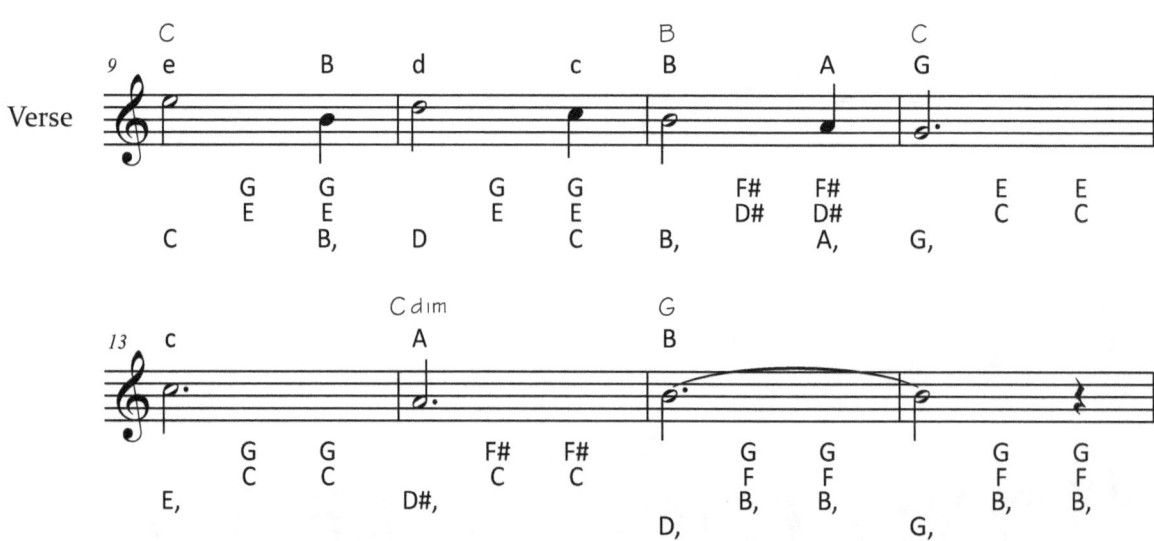

Officially known as "Pomp and Circumstance", this was composed by Sir Edward Elgar in 1901. Notated here from the Jeffries Duet playing of Hidetoshi Yamashita (see Videos & Recordings).

Land of Hope & Glory

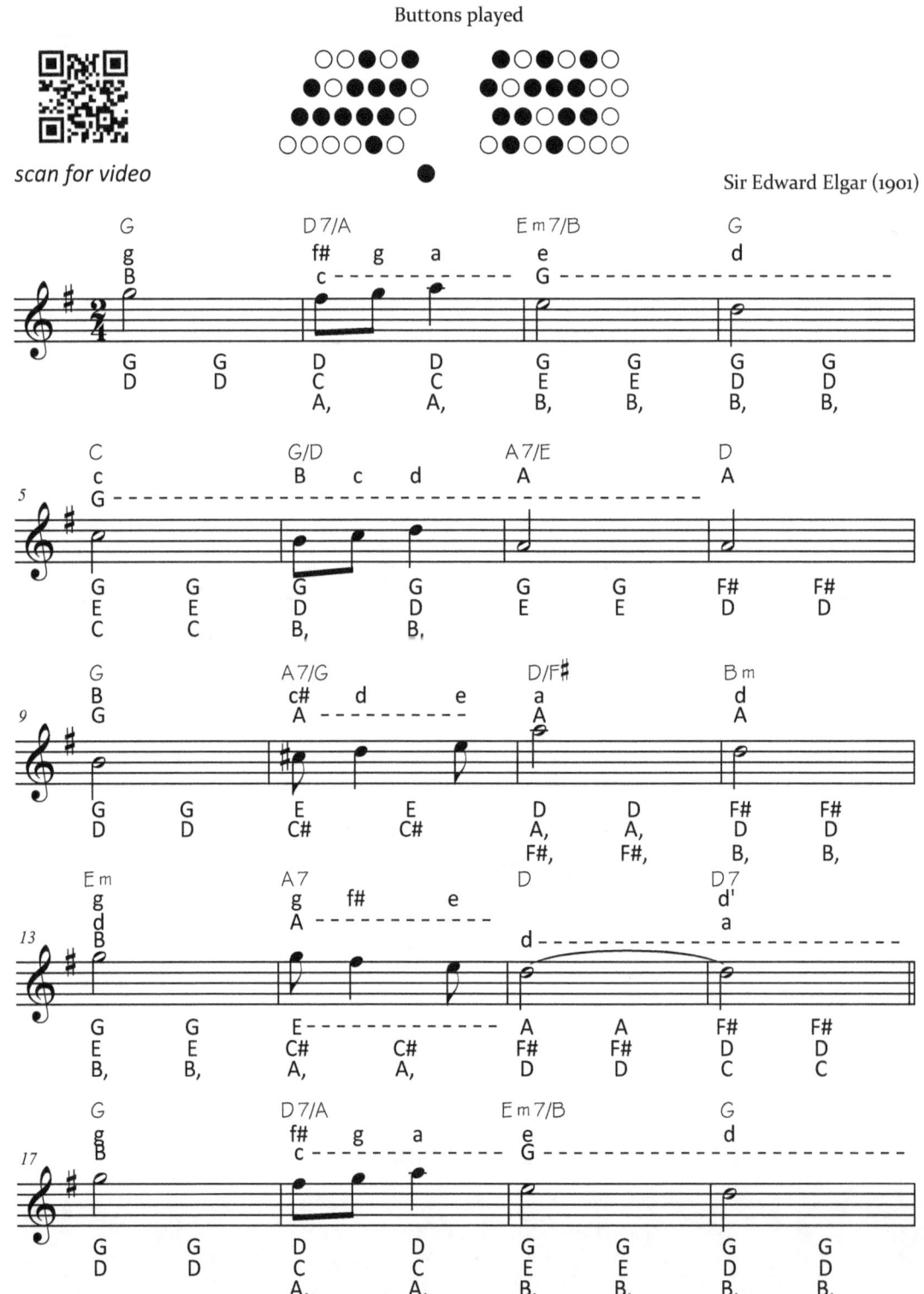

Sir Edward Elgar (1901)

Composed by Scott Joplin in 1902, this tune became incredibly popular after being featured in the 1973 Paul Newman/Robert Redford film "The Sting". The first two sections are notated here in the original key of C.

The Entertainer

A plaintive farewell ballad from World War I, with music composed by Ernest R. Ball and lyrics by J. Keirn Brennan.

Goodbye, Good Luck, God Bless You

The Jeffries Duet Concertina Tutor

A classic Tin Pan Alley Song (and title) very popular during World War I, composed by J. Fred Helf in 1906. It was also recorded by Jimmie Davis, the prolific "Singing Governor" of Louisiana.

When You Know You're Not Forgotten by the Girl You Can't Forget

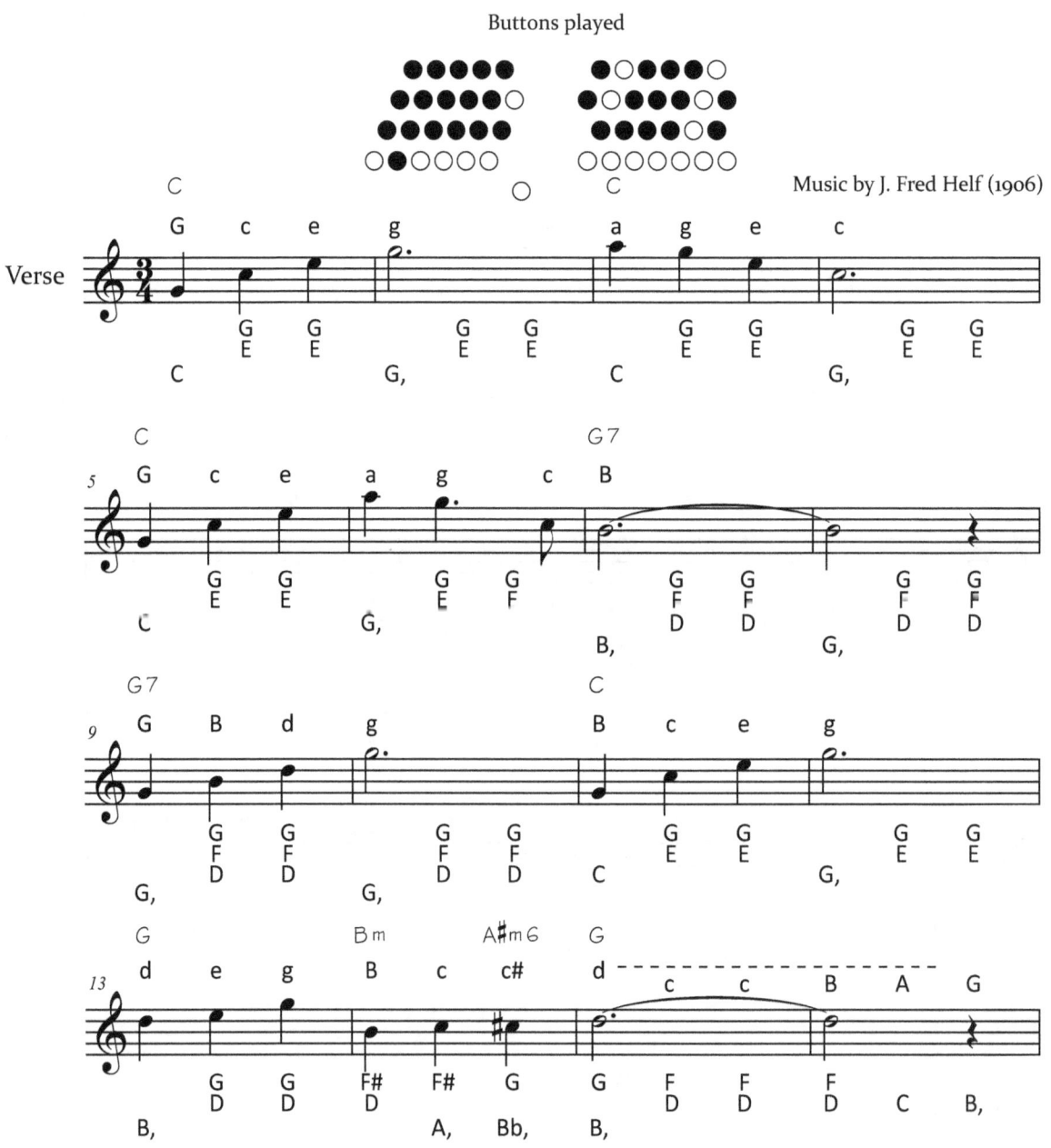

156   The Jeffries Duet Concertina Tutor

Page 154 of *The Methodist Hymnal* (1939), transposed note-for-note to the key of G.

Christ the Lord is Risen Today

Officially titled "Bagatelle No. 25 in A Minor" by Ludwig van Beethoven in 1810, and only discovered in 1867, forty years after his death. The identity of "Elise" is a mystery.

Fur Elise

"Dutch" is an affectionate London slang term for wife or mother, deriving from "Duchess". Recorded by Albert Chevalier in 1912, Peter Sellers in 1959 and Herman's Hermits in 1966. And, also recorded by Michael Hebbert on his 1976 album *The Rampin' Cat*.

My Old Dutch

Music by Charles Ingle (1892)

Composed by American bandleader John Philip Sousa in 1893 and perhaps better known as the opening theme for the famous 1970's British comedy TV show "Monty Python's Flying Circus".

The Liberty Bell March

Buttons played

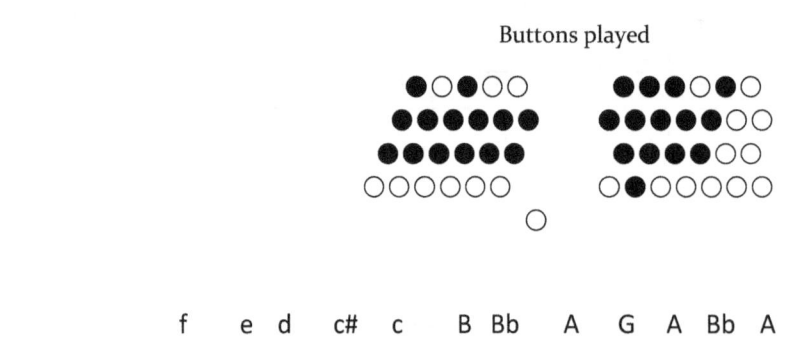

John Philip Sousa (1893)

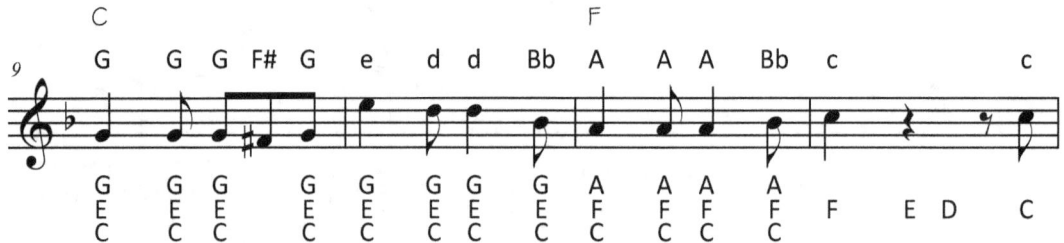

Mistakenly labeled "The Merry Month of May" on *The Rampin' Cat*, this tune is actually a Scottish reel called "The Cross of Inverness" (Clach na Cudain) first published in 1816.

The Cross of Inverness

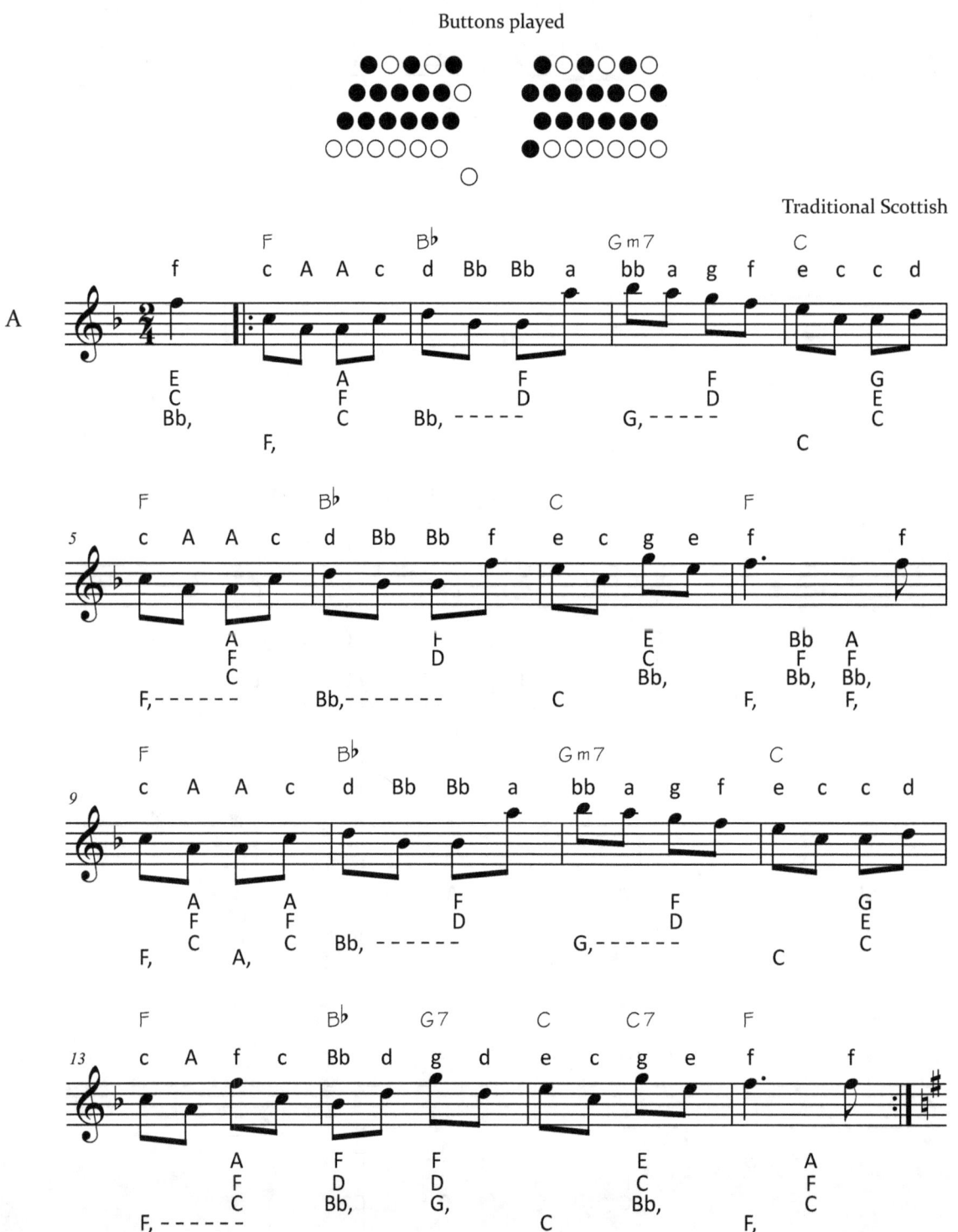

Traditional Scottish

The Jeffries Duet Concertina Tutor

A popular British Music Hall song composed by John H. Glover-Kind in 1907. It is featured on *The Rampin' Cat* with vocals by Andrew Frank.

I Do Like to be Beside the Seaside

Written by African-American songwriter, singer and pianist Turner Layton, and recorded by Sophie Tucker, Bessie Smith, Louis Armstrong, Bing Crosby, Fats Waller, Duke Ellington, Benny Goodman, Django Reinhardt, Al Jolson, Tony Bennet, Judy Garland, Ella Fitzgerald, Peggy Lee, Bobby Darin, Nina Simone, Mel Torme, Chet Atkins, Frank Sinatra...

After You've Gone

A traditional waltz from Venezuela, learned from the playing of the Hotpoint Stringband on *The Road to Burhania* album.

La Partida

Traditional Venezuelan

The Jeffries Duet Concertina Tutor

This is the fifth movement from Johann Sebastian Bach's Suite in E minor for Lute, BWV 996. (See "Videos & Recordings" section to hear it played on Jeffries Duet by Gavin Atkin). If you want, you can even jazz it up like Jethro Tull's Ian Anderson did on their *Stand Up* album.

Bourrée in E minor

A beautifully moody and romantic tune from French composer Gabriel Faure. Play it slowly and expressively.

Pavane

Gabriel Faure, 1887

When international singing superstar Enrico Caruso died in 1921 at age 48, the entire world went into mourning and George Little teamed up with Jack Stanley to pen this song which sold more than two million copies of sheet music. Notated here from Michael Hebbert's *The Rampin' Cat*.

They Needed a Songbird in Heaven
(So God Took Caruso Away)

The Jeffries Duet Concertina Tutor

From the *Notebook for Anna Magdalena Bach* dated 1725. Titled the "Minuet in D Minor" (BWV Anh. 132), it is transposed here to G Minor to better fit the 50-button Jeffries Duet with a home key of C. And so we can finish with that lowest bottom G note.

Minuet in D Minor

(in G Minor)

Buttons played

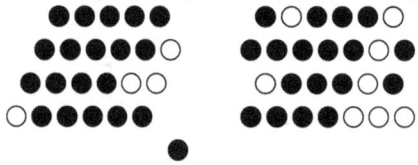

J.S. Bach (1722)

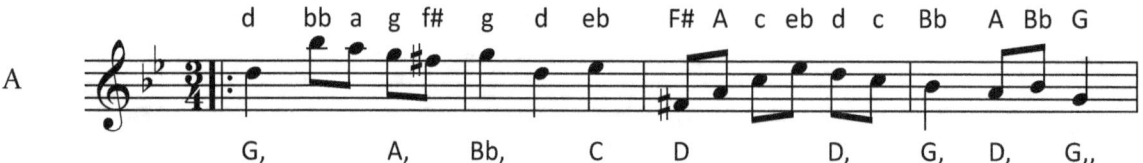

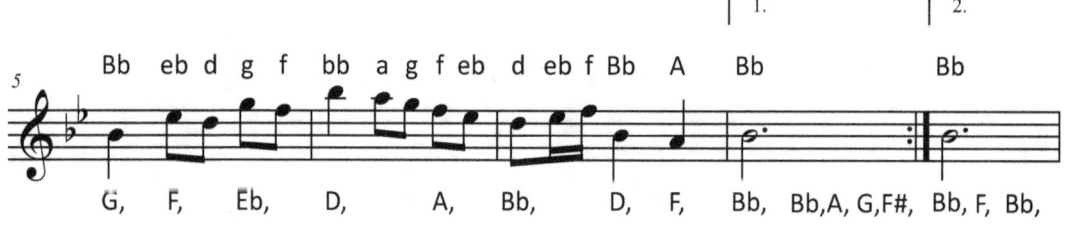

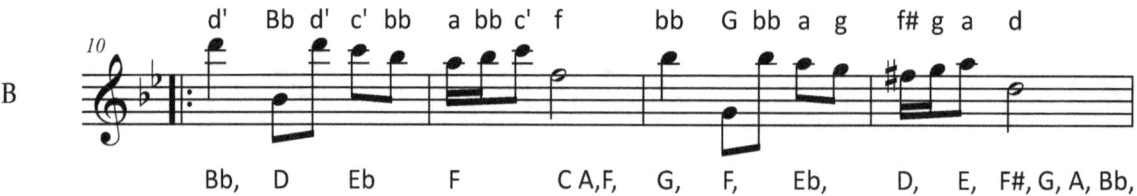

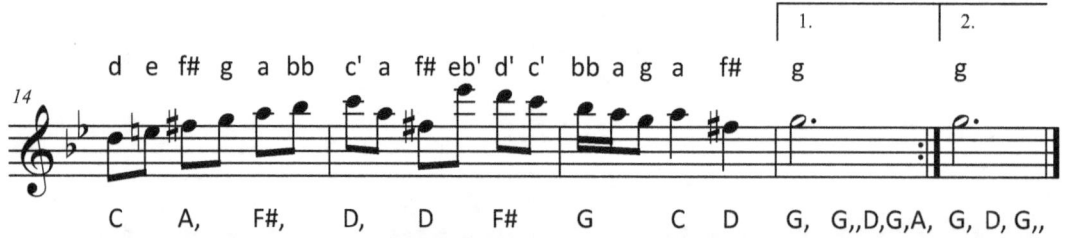

The Jeffries Duet Concertina Tutor

VIDEOS & RECORDINGS

 "Jeffries Duet" playlist on *Angloconc* YouTube channel

Michael Hebbert

 https://youtu.be/6uRWxvLW2hA

Sueño de Juventud
Avalon
South Georgia Whaling Song
Sunny Side of the Street

 https://youtu.be/iGwFWD90U0Q

(At Swaledale Squeeze 2012)

 https://youtu.be/_1JxYMjUA9o

(Bampton English Country Music Weekend 2015)

 https://youtu.be/GAqBG8GFbVI

Appelbo Gånglåt
Fanteladda
Lappkungens Polska
Slängpolska efter Byss-Calle No.32

 https://youtu.be/ofy72oHuJ9w

Lull Me Beyond Thee
Jack's Health
Wooden Shoes
Hole in the Wall
Bonnie Grey-Ey'd Morn

   https://soundcloud.com/michael-hebbert

Oscar Wood's Waltz	The Whim
Sweet England	Jack's Maggot
Oakpit Waltz	Jack's Health
Anos Dourados	Mad Dick
Sueño de Juventud	Holborn March
Hasta Morir (Venezuelan Waltz)	An Ataireachd Ard (The Surge of the Sea)
Don't Dilly-Dally On The Way	Alfonsina y el Mar
She Was One Of The Early Birds (& I Was One Of The Worms)	Diarmuid's March
	Ar Eirinn
Daring Young Man On The Flying Trapeze	St Sechnall
Barney Google	Lagan Love
Daddy Wouldn't Buy Me A Bow-Wow	They'll Never Believe Me
The Boy I Love Is Up In The Gallery	Maybe It's Because I'm A Londoner
Hinei Ma Tov	

THE RAMPIN' CAT

The Rampin' Cat: Songs, Ballads, and English Country Dance Tunes, Played on the Jeffries Duet Concertina (Free Reed FRR009, 1977)

Stuart Estell

https://youtu.be/6JiyQSDynfg

Half a Person

https://youtu.be/v2shFQAVjjM

Lucy Wan

https://youtu.be/cRNpuaUKKoo

You Only Tell Me You Love Me When You're Drunk

https://youtu.be/FZppwAy9_2k

The Courting Coat

https://soundcloud.com/lachenaliamusic/ouroboros-is-broken-concertina

Ouroboros is Broken

https://soundcloud.com/lachenaliamusic/grandstand

Theme from Grandstand

https://soundcloud.com/lachenaliamusic/the-elf-princess

The Elf Princess

https://soundcloud.com/lachenaliamusic/clyde-water-the-mothers-malison-roud-91-child-216

Clyde Water

 https://soundcloud.com/lachenaliamusic/elizabeth-my-dear-stone-roses-cover

Elizabeth My Dear

 https://soundcloud.com/lachenaliamusic/lady-margaret-and-sweet-william

Lady Margaret and Sweet William

 https://soundcloud.com/lachenaliamusic/the-prickleye-bush

The Prickleye Bush

 https://soundcloud.com/lachenaliamusic/the-haymakers

The Haymakers

 https://soundcloud.com/earth-recordings/stewart-lee-and-stuart-estell

Polly on the Shore

 https://soundcloud.com/lachenaliamusic/billy-again-part-1-concertina-and-piano

Billy Again – Part 1

 https://soundcloud.com/lachenaliamusic/da-slockit-light

Da Slockit Light

Nick Robertshaw

https://youtu.be/zUTcMOYqllA
Beer That Tastes Like Beer

https://youtu.be/ARYbZZq_aeo
Hellship

https://youtu.be/KKRbR_LUxSs
Medley

https://youtu.be/AbahVkzohoY
Hot Meat

https://youtu.be/pIBofoFpap0
Planxty Fanny Power

http://rememberbignick.pbworks.com/w/page/10496931/A%20Night%20with%20Big%20Nick

GAVIN ATKIN

https://youtu.be/NT1rsn4SUls

Underneath the Arches
Don't Get Around Much Anymore
The Lambeth Walk
Maybe It's Because I'm a Londoner

https://youtu.be/z3ViKA9ot88

I'm Going to Sit Right Down and Write Myself a Letter

Photo by Ewan Ryan-Atkin

https://youtu.be/YCiYD3OwEgE

Teddy Bear's Picnic

https://youtu.be/3F_Cs6tzx_U

On a Slow Boat to China

https://youtu.be/mdTaIp1sGvk

Bourée

SENTIMENTAL JOURNEY, Julie & Gavin Atkin, Red Admiral Records (2013)

Tracks with Jeffries Duet:

Sentimental Journey
The Glory of Love
Ain't Misbehavin'
How Much Is That Doggie in the Window
I'm Gonna Sit Right Down and Write Myself A Letter
It's a Sin to Tell a Lie
Memphis in June
Moonlight Serenade
My Happiness
On A Slow Boat to China
Two Sleepy People
Everything Stops for Tea
A Nightingale Sang in Berkeley Square

Hidetoshi Yamashita

https://youtu.be/nZDouTLPwVg
My Way

https://youtu.be/CCmXyu4-2V8
Air on G String

https://youtu.be/I9oTTBSKb9M
Land of Hope and Glory

https://youtu.be/VlblsBQh-3k
Live for Life

https://youtu.be/4a7OxlPDECM
Jesu Joy of Man's Desiring

https://youtu.be/rDgOWmpzvkI
As Time Goes By

https://youtu.be/k-ewDXdn8A0
Air on a G string in D Minor

Peter Trimming

https://youtu.be/eZ8_gBmii1A
Marche des Cabrettaires

https://youtu.be/JCAK0GTOFf4
Bourree d'Egletons

https://youtu.be/GI86PWlB_cM
Cancion de Cuna

Gary Coover

https://youtu.be/UPijYeCqwAo
Galopede / Mr & Mrs Mickey Mouse

Paul Woloschuk

https://youtu.be/WnQJeMFrNn4
Dundas

Marien Lina

https://youtu.be/F0NrTS75bbk
Het Verdwaalde Paasei (The Lost Easter Egg)

The Jeffries Duet Concertina Tutor

THE AUTHOR

GARY COOVER has enjoyed and played traditional British Isles folk music for many many years ever since stumbling upon the music of Steeleye Span and the "Morris On" and "Son of Morris On" LP's while in college.

For over 15 years Gary hosted and produced the popular "Shepherd's Hey" radio program of British Isles traditional music on KPFT FM-90.1 in Houston, Texas. He was a founding band member of "The Four Bricks out of Hadrian's Wall" where he played concertina, melodeon, keyboards and bass. He also danced position "#5" in the Men of Houston Morris Dance team.

Gary has published numerous instruction books for the Anglo concertina, and in addition to Anglo and Jeffries Duet plays English concertina and melodeon.

  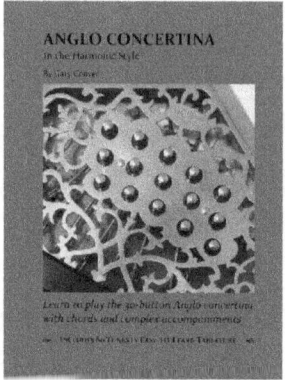 

   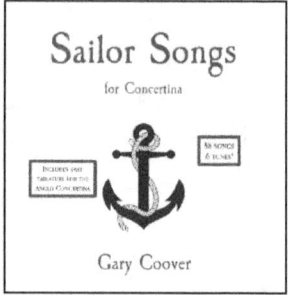

ACKNOWLEDGEMENTS & THANKS

Charles Jeffries for enriching the musical and concertina world by inventing this unusual "Anglo-German" duet and for making such high-quality instruments that so many are still in top playing form today over a hundred years later.

Michael Hebbert for his landmark recording *The Rampin' Cat*, the first-ever album that featured the Jeffries Duet concertina, showing what incredible arrangements and musicianship sound like on this unique instrument. And for being so gracious and helpful and allowing several of his arrangements to be included in this book.

Erik House for photographs and tunes in keys outside the home key, **Paul Woloschuk** for the beautiful photograph on the cover, **Hidetoshi Yamashita** for photographs and arrangements, **Gavin Atkin** for photos and advice, **Rod Wagoner** for photographs of his Jeffries Duet, **Gavin Davenport** for photographs of his converted Jeffries Duet, **Geoffrey Crabb** for dates of manufacture for Crabb Jeffries Duets, **Chris Algar** for help with determining historical sales of Jeffries Duets, **Luke Hobbs** for a photograph of a large Jeffries Duet at an estate auction, and **Nigel Sture** and **Steve Turner** for photographs of an unusual 27-button mini Jeffries Duet.

The late **Nick Robertshaw** for truly being a "larger-than-life" concertina player and tireless promoter and player of the Jeffries Duet, and whose wife, Terry, kindly gave permission to include two of his songs and arrangements of tunes he played.

The **Shetland Musical Heritage Trust**, **Jody Kruskal**, **Dave Leggett** and **Steve Hartz** for permission to include tunes currently in copyright.

Neil Wayne for all his efforts that helped create the Concertina Revival of the 1970's, including collecting an astonishing number of historical instruments, publishing Free Reed Magazine, and recording so many concertina artists on the Free Reed Label. *And for selling me a Jeffries Duet!*

Robert Gaskins for his diligent research into all things concertina and for the scholarly website concertina.com.

Paul Schwartz for creating and shepherding the incredibly helpful and informative online forum found at www.concertina.net.

And especially **Greg Jowaisas**, for all his efforts to restore Jeffries Duets and keep them in good playing condition, for sharing some really beautiful photos, and because he asked politely and persisted doggedly over so many years for a tutor to explain and teach this unusual little bellows-powered music-making machine.

For more information on Charles Jeffries and his concertinas:

www.concertina.com/jeffries/concertina-maker/index.htm
www.concertinajournal.org/articles/charles-jeffries-and-his-sons/
www.concertina.com/jeffries/man-and-family/index.htm
www.concertina.com/jeffries-duet/index.htm
www.concertinajournal.org
www.concertina.net

ALPHABETICAL LIST OF TUNES

A Mighty Fortress is Our God 102
After You've Gone 170
Alfred Montmarquette's 6/8 76
Amazing Grace 46
American Boot Dance 88
American Patrol 116
Angeline the Baker (C) 119
Angeline the Baker (D) 118
Auld Donald 110
Auld Lang Syne 58
Battle of the Somme 95
Beer That Tastes Like Beer 134
Blue-Eyed Stranger 59
Bourrée in E minor 174
Christ the Lord is Risen Today 158
Country Gardens 78
Cowman's Prayer 55
Cross of Inverness 164
Da Slockit Light 86
Dearest Dickie 94
Eleanor Plunkett 82
Entertainer 148
Flow Gently Sweet Afton 45
Frere Jacques 40
Fur Elise 159
Furusato 53
Galopede 66
Gärdebylåten 100
Gathering Peascods 114
Goodbye, Good Luck, God Bless You 150
Gurnard Waltz 74
Hell Ship 104
How Great Thou Art 123
I Do Like to be Beside the Seaside 166
In Dulci Jubilo 80
In the Bleak Midwinter 68
Indian Queen 109
Kate's Rambles 73
King Pharim 52
Kojo no Tsuki 132
La Partida 172
Land of Hope & Glory 146
Let Me Call You Sweetheart 142
Liberty Bell March 162

Title	Page
Loch Lomond	69
Logan Water	44
Londonderry Air	103
Man in the Moon	50
Mary Had a Little Lamb	35
Merry Month of May	97
Minuet in D Minor	182
Minuet in G	122
Miss Smith's Morris	64
Mudgee Waltz	81
My Old Dutch	160
My Wild Irish Rose	124
Nottingham Castle	133
Oh Susanna (chords)	47
Oh Susanna	38
Old Magnolia	96
Orkney Rope Waltz	120
Pavane	176
Peter's Peerie Boat	90
Poor Old Horse (C)	36
Poor Old Horse (G)	37
Pop Goes the Weasel	41
Portsmouth (Setting 1)	106
Portsmouth (Setting 2)	108
Procrastination Waltz	92
Quaker's Wife	72
Queen's Delight	84
Red Wing	98
Rights of Man	83
Rose of the Redlands	56
Salmontails Up the Water	70
Shenandoah	79
St. James Infirmary	140
Star of the County Down	62
They Needed a Songbird in Heaven	179
Three Around Three	111
Twinkle Twinkle Little Star	39
Under the Anheuser Busch	136
Variations on Shepherd's Hey	42
Weeping, Sad and Lonely	60
Whaleman's Lament	54
What a Friend We Have in Jesus	112
When Irish Eyes Are Smiling	128
When You Know You're Not Forgotten by the Girl You Can't Forget	154
Young Collins	48

LOOKING FOR A JEFFRIES DUET?

Jeffries Duets have not been made for over 50 years, but with luck you will be able to find a vintage instrument in good playing condition from these fine folks in the US and UK:

Greg Jowaisas

"Concertina Repairman of Note"

Concertinas tuned, repaired, refurbished

English, Anglo and Duet

Jeffries Duets a specialty and in stock

521 Forest View Lane
Taylor Mill, KY 41015
gjowaisas@fioptics.com
(859) 803-9472

BARLEYCORN CONCERTINAS

Purveyors of fine concertinas & folk instruments since 1972

Over the last 40 years, thousands of instruments have reached the hands of players from our company and we boast some of the greatest exponents of the instrument among our customers.

As the largest stockist of concertinas in the world, we are at your service and we can undoubtedly find the instrument you are seeking...
From beginner's boxes to the finest instruments from the golden age of concertina manufacture, Barleycorn has the concertina for you!

Phone: +44 (0)1270 879958
Email: barleycorn@concertina.co.uk
Web: http://www.concertina.co.uk

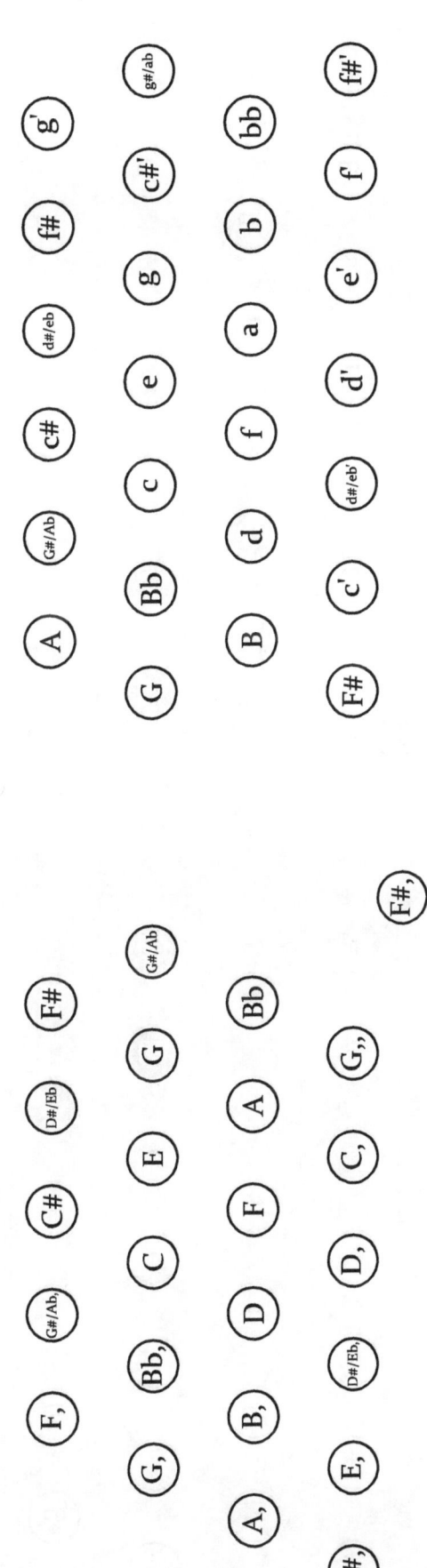

The Jeffries Duet Concertina Tutor

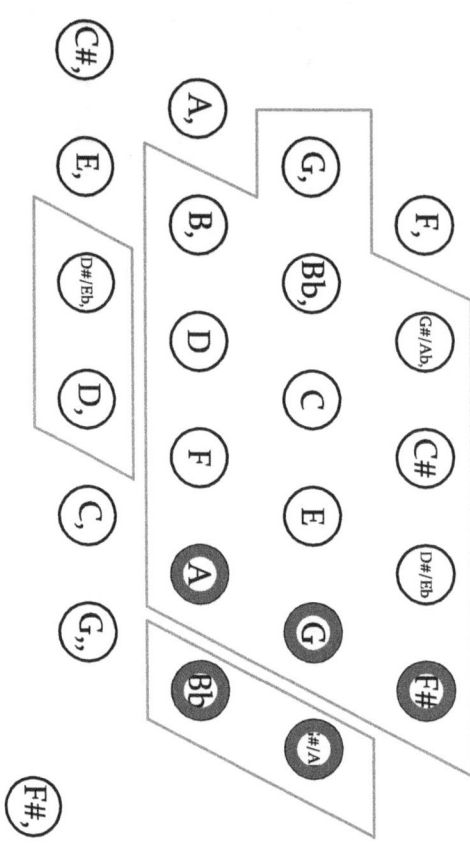
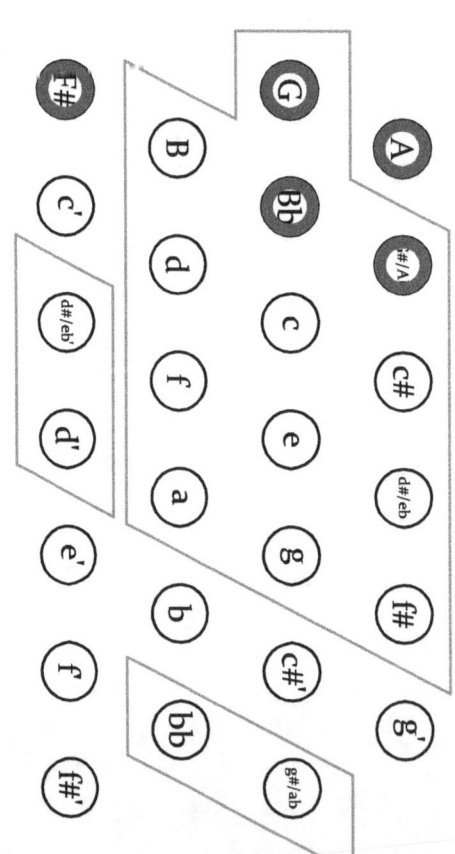

The Jeffries Duet Concertina Tutor

www.ingramcontent.com/pod-product-compliance
Lightning Source LLC
Chambersburg PA
CBHW080550230426
43663CB00015B/2781